THE EPIC OF MOUNT EVEREST

Sir Francis Younghusband was one of Britain's most famous nineteenth-century explorers, discovering a new land route from China to India. In 1903 he led a military expedition to Tibet, and in later life was the organizer of the first attempts to climb Mount Everest. He died in 1942.

Patrick French is the author of *Younghusband: The Last Great Imperial Adventurer*, which won the Somerset Maugham Award and the Royal Society of Literature Heinemann Prize.

Sir Francis Younghusband

THE EPIC OF
MOUNT EVEREST

PAN BOOKS

First published 1926 by Edward Arnold & Co.

This edition published 2000 by Pan Books
an imprint of Macmillan Publishers Ltd
25 Eccleston Place, London SW1W 9NF,
Basingstoke and Oxford
Associated companies throughout the world
www.macmillan.com

ISBN 0 330 48285 8

1 3 5 7 9 8 6 4 2

A CIP catalogue record for this book is available from
the British Library.

Typeset by SX Composing DTP, Rayleigh, Essex
Printed and bound in Great Britain by
Mackays of Chatham plc, Chatham, Kent

CONTENTS

PREFACE

Separate descriptions of the three Mount Everest expeditions have already been written by those who took part in them, and have been published in the three books, *Mount Everest: The Reconnaissance*, 1921; *The Assault on Mount Everest*, 1922; and *The Fight for Everest*, 1924. The present volume purports to be a condensed description of the three expeditions. It is written on behalf of the Mount Everest Committee, and is based on the above-named publications. For the sake of connectedness and brevity of narrative the exact words of the previous writers are not always used; but they are followed as closely as may be, and the present writer freely and gratefully acknowledges his indebtedness to those who have brought back such vivid accounts of their exploits.

F. E. Y.
June, 1926.

NOTE

As the following pages are going through the press comes the news – too late for insertion in the body of this book – that Dr J. S. Haldane, in a lecture to the physiological section of the British Association at Oxford on acclimatization to high altitudes, said that the new physiological facts elicited by the Mount Everest expeditions were of the most striking character. It was shown that acclimatization sufficient to prevent any symptom of mountain sickness could be obtained at a height of even 27,000 feet. The experiences of Norton, Somervell, and Odell on that point were conclusive. To an unacclimatized person a stay of any duration at a height of 27,000 feet would have meant absolutely certain death. He accounted for the acclimatization on Mount Everest by assuming that the lungs actively secreted oxygen inwards.

F. E. Y.
August, 1926.

LIST OF ILLUSTRATIONS

IX

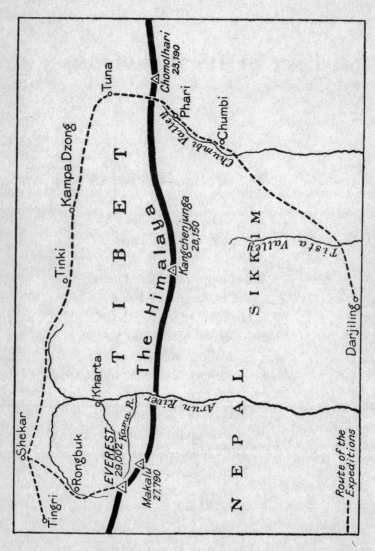

The Route Followed By The Expeditions

INTRODUCTION

by Patrick French

The discovery of George Leigh Mallory's alabaster corpse, high on the slopes of Everest in the summer of 1999, had a spectacular universal impact. Books, articles and television programmes appeared, as the debate was revived about whether he had reached the summit seventy-five years before. Mallory – his physical grace, the manner of his disappearance, the era in which he lived – will always hold the public's attention. He is the emblem of the early Everest expeditions, when relays of British males tried to climb the highest mountain in the world. George Bernard Shaw likened the spectacle to a picnic in Connemara surprised by a snowstorm.

An international team of climbers went in search of George Mallory and Sandy Irvine. The hope was that by finding their bodies, and possibly the Kodak Vestpocket camera they were known to be carrying, the mystery of whether they made it to the summit three decades before Tenzing Norgay and Edmund Hillary might be solved. Aided by careful advance research and good luck, the climbers found a frozen corpse high on the mountain, perfectly preserved from 1924. It was the body of an athlete, lying face down at full stretch, the right leg broken, fingers gripping the frozen gravel in a desperate attempt to slide no further. He was wearing hobnail boots and a leather motorcycling helmet, a torn flannel shirt and a woollen jersey, and a frayed rope was looped round his middle. There was a schoolmaster's name tape on the shirt collar – G. Mallory.

There was no camera, but by analysing notes in his pockets and other fresh data, his discoverers concluded that the probability of a successful summit was greater than previously thought. The mystery remains, with the elusive camera and its cold, undeveloped film being the only way a definitive answer might ever be found.

Francis Younghusband, the author of *The Epic of Mount Everest*, was the promoter and instigator of the first four sustained assaults on the mountain. He was also, according to a frequently repeated story, the inventor of the very idea of trying to stand on the top. He is said to have had this notion in the early 1890s while climbing near Chitral with Charles 'Bruiser' Bruce, a leading figure in the early expeditions. Whether the story is true is doubtful. In 1932, Younghusband wrote in a letter to his daughter, Eileen:

> I had Charlie Bruce to lunch today and we had a real good crack ... He has a yarn that I had a scheme forty years ago for him & me to go up Everest and that I have thought of nothing ever since! He is going to write an article about it for the Daily Telegraph and if it brings in another twenty quid to the Expedition funds that is all to the good.

The funding of mountaineering expeditions has remained a constant anxiety, and is, indirectly, the cause of much of the present fascination with Mount Everest.

In 1996, in a disaster that had long been anticipated, nine people died near the summit in a matter of days, and several more were permanently disfigured. Most were on commercial expeditions, either as guides or as clients. The higher reaches of the mountain were crowded with climbers who were not qualified to be there.

There was great bitterness in the aftermath. A journalist who had accompanied the 'Adventure Consultants' team, Jon Krakauer, wrote *Into Thin Air*, an instant account of the debacle which soon became an international bestseller, feeding the growing public hunger in affluent societies for true stories of extreme human discomfort. It offered a vivid picture of the jealousy and feuding both between and within the teams, and the pernicious influence of people with enough money to get to the top of the world, but no sustained mountaineering experience. His book contained some unforgettable descriptions: the New York socialite Sandy Hill Pittman being hauled up the mountain on a tether by a young Sherpa guide; the long dead climbers, or rather the bits of long dead climbers, that litter the slopes; the mental derangement caused by sustained oxygen deprivation at high altitude; and the terrible image of the climber Rob Hall, trapped and frostbitten on the summit ridge, dying on the end of a satellite phone. 'I love you. Sleep well, my sweetheart. Please don't worry too much,' were his last recorded words, spoken to his wife in New Zealand.

As often happens in such cases, the leader of the pack soon had detractors snapping at his heels, and Krakauer was accused of writing a distorted, self-serving account. The Russian climber Anatoli Boukreev, a guide on the rival 'Mountain Madness' team, produced *The Climb*, a ghostwritten book which offered an alternative interpretation of events, only to die before publication in an avalanche on Annapurna. Much of the conflict, appropriately enough for a pursuit that has been transformed by developments in electronic technology, was fought on the pages of online magazines and web sites, each riposte drawing a further riposte.

Feuds and recriminations have long been a feature of high-altitude mountaineering expeditions. When people are cramped together in freezing conditions for months on end, and a misjudgement can provoke disaster or death, discord is inevitable. In *Ghosts of Everest*, the 'official' account of the 1999 search for Mallory and Irvine, the authors enjoy detailing their disputes with Peter Firstbrook, who made a film of the expedition for the BBC and wrote a slapdash competing account, *Lost on Everest*. In the 1920s, there was antagonism not only between individuals, but between the organizing committee, made up of Royal Geographical Society and Alpine Club stalwarts and the climbers out on the mountain. 'I sometimes think of this expedition as a fraud from beginning to end,' wrote Mallory from the slopes of Everest, 'invented by the wild enthusiasm of one man, Younghusband; puffed up by the would-be wisdom of certain pundits in the Alpine Club; and imposed upon the youthful ardour of your humble servant.'

In other respects, life as a mountaineer was markedly different in the 1920s. As Mallory said, the early Everesters had to 'walk off the map'. Before the 1921 reconnaissance expedition, nobody had ever climbed much beyond 24,000 feet. The summit was known to be at least another 5,000 feet beyond the clouds. Scientific knowledge of acclimatization and the effects of sustained oxygen deprivation was minimal. There were no satellite phones, no global positioning systems, no helicopters, no ergonomic jackets. Several of the climbers were consummate amateurs: the leader of the 1921 expedition, Colonel Howard Bury, appears to have been chosen because, in Younghusband's words, he 'had done a good deal of shooting, both in the Alps and the Himalaya' and 'knew how to deal with Asiatics'.

What is extraordinary, in retrospect, is the scale of their achievement. Edward Norton, who led the 1924 expedition, was an army officer known primarily for organizing a pig-sticking competition called the Kadir Cup. Leaving London for Everest:

> It was not much more than a minute before the train left Victoria that he arrived at the station on his way to India and he was leisurely saying goodbye to his friends and the train was well on the move as he quietly stepped into it continuing his conversation.

Yet Norton climbed to within 900 feet of the summit without supplementary oxygen, wearing 'a lightish knickerbocker suit of windproof gaberdine' and leather-soled felt boots. As one member of the 1999 expedition remarked after finding Mallory's body: 'Hell, I walk out on the street at Seattle with more clothing than he had on at 28,000 feet on Everest!'

To an extent, this success can be pinned on the pace at which the early expeditions proceeded. There was a slow sea voyage from England and a long trek from Darjiling to the base of the mountain to acclimatize and build up stamina. There was time to inspect the birds and flowers of Sikkim and the Chumbi Valley ('And in the forest were great bushes, eight to ten feet in height, of *R. cinnabarinum* which is here at its best and varied in shade from yellow and orange to deep red'). Unlike today, there were no commercial pressures from sponsors or clients to reach the top, only an individual's determination. At this time, particularly among those who had been through the rigours of the First World War, there was also an ingrained expectation of hardship, cold and physical discomfort.

Francis Younghusband wrote *The Epic of Mount Everest* – the definitive account of the 1921, 1922 and 1924 expeditions – in the aftermath of Mallory and Irvine's death, when it was not clear whether a further attempt on the mountain would ever be permitted. The Tibetan government had been angered by the frivolous captions attached to a jerky film shot high on the mountain, and so had refused to sanction any further ascents.

Born in India, Younghusband made his reputation as a spy and explorer in China and Central Asia, and led the 1903 British invasion of Tibet. Although he had the outward bearing of a late Victorian imperial servant, an outlandish heart beat within him. By his later years, he was endorsing Indian nationalism, writing books about translucent extraterrestrials who communicated by ether waves, and thought he was about to father 'a God-Child who will manifest God more completely even than Jesus did'. For him, the Everest expeditions were, in Mallory's words, 'a sort of religious pilgrimage . . . Younghusband amuses and delights me more than anything – grim old apostle of beauty and adventure'. The compliment was returned, Mallory being described in these pages as, 'certainly good-looking, with a sensible, cultivated air . . . slim and supple, if not broad and beefy', a view only slightly less restrained than the essayist Lytton Strachey's famous, 'Mon Dieu! – George Mallory! –

When that's been written, what more need be said? . . . he's six foot high, with the body of an athlete by Praxiteles, and a face – oh incredible . . .'

Younghusband was convinced that climbing mountains was an instinctive human urge, despite being, in practical terms, of 'no more use than kicking a football about, or dancing, or playing the piano, or writing a poem, or painting a picture'; a view not far from Mallory's famous 'because it is there' justification. It is an opinion that might be compared with the reaction of Ngawang Tenzin Norbu, the head monk of Rongbuk Monastery, when he heard that seven Sherpa porters had been killed in an avalanche during the 1922 expedition: 'I was filled with great compassion that they underwent such suffering in unnecessary work.'

The Epic of Mount Everest is set firmly in the era in which it was written. Despite his eccentricities, Younghusband, who when he wrote it was in his sixties, had the social and racial assumptions of his time. The sphere in which he differed from other early promoters of climbing Everest was in his quasi-mystical emphasis on the lure and power of the mountain, rather than the geographical or scientific benefits that might come from an ascent.

> Knowledge is not everything in life. Science may be satisfied, but the soul is not. It was the spirit, not science, that embarked upon this enterprise. And the spirit can never rest satisfied until it is completed.

Having spent prolonged periods of his life in hazardous conditions, in Tibet, the Karakorums and the Pamirs, Younghusband was aware of what he was encouraging others to do. For him, the pursuit of physical extremes was mentally and spiritually beneficial, and the risks were incidental. Although he would have disapproved of the cluttering of remote landscapes with people and equipment, he would have been in no way surprised at the enduring obsession with climbing high peaks. Centuries pass, mountaineers pass, but Everest remains, an impassive killer, drawing people upward.

Patrick French

Chapter One

THE IDEA

That Mount Everest is the highest mountain in the world, and 29,002 feet in height, everybody knows. And most people know also that in attempting to climb the mountain two Englishmen lost their lives; that these two, Mallory and Irvine, were 'last seen going strong for the top'; and that the top being only 800 feet away they must have very nearly, perhaps actually, reached it.

How this was done; and how Norton, without oxygen, reached an altitude of 28,100 feet, and his companion, Somervell, scarcely a hundred feet less; how Odell, also without oxygen, twice reached a height of 27,000 feet, and might well have reached the summit itself if more porters had been available; how these feats were made possible by Himalayan porters carrying loads to nearly 27,000 feet; and how all this was done after the expedition had suffered from a blizzard of exceptional severity and cold as low as 24 degrees below zero at an altitude of 21,000 feet, and, most remarkable of all, after Norton, Somervell and Mallory had been drained of the best part of their resources through having to turn back and rescue four Himalayan porters marooned on a glacier at 23,000 feet; is the story now to be told.

And first as to the idea these men had in their minds – the idea of climbing Mount Everest.

When we see a hill we are sooner or later driven to try and get to the top of it. We cannot let it stand there for ever without our scrambling up it. Partly this is because we would like to see the view from the top. But more especially is it because the hill presents a challenge to us. We must match ourselves against it and show that we *can* get to the top – show ourselves and show our neighbours. We like to show ourselves off – display our prowess. It is an exertion to get to the top, but we enjoy making it. We are doing something that makes us proud of ourselves and gives us inner satisfaction.

But when we first look at Mount Everest it is a very different proposition. To get to the top of *that* we never dream. It is right up in the skies – far beyond human reach. So it seems to us. And hundreds of millions of Indians have through the ages looked up at the great Himalayan peaks and not dared to think of climbing even the minor giants, much less the monarch of them all. They will patiently suffer most terrible hardships in travelling thinly clad from the hot plains of India to some place of pilgrimage by a glacier in the Himalaya. Of sheer suffering they will endure as much as any Everest climber. But even the *idea* of climbing the great peaks never comes into their heads. Not even to those hardy people who spend their whole lives in the mountains has it come. That they have the physical capacity to get to the top of the very highest is proved by the fact they carried loads to nearly 27,000 feet in 1924. And if they could carry a load to that height presumably they could go unloaded to 29,000 feet. Still the idea of climbing Mount Everest they have never entertained.

How then is it that islanders from the North Sea should have thought of such a thing? Far back we owe the inspiration to the Swiss and Italians. The Alpine peaks are only about half the height of the Himalayan giants. But even they had been looked on with dread and horror till at the end of the eighteenth century the Swiss De Saussure and the Italian Placidus à Spescha tackled their highest summits. The climbers groaned and puffed and panted and suffered from headaches and sickness. Still they attained the summit. And once the highest mountain in the Alps had been conquered the lesser peaks also fell. And soon we English were following in De Saussure's steps. Through all last century we were engaged in conquering the Alps. And when they were well subdued we turned to higher game. Douglas Freshfield climbed the highest peak in the Caucasus. And Martin Conway the highest in the Andes. Italians also joined in the struggle. The Duke of the Abruzzi climbed Ruwenzori in East Africa and Mount St Elias in Alaska.

Ambition grew with success. The Alps, the Caucasus and the Andes had been conquered. And men were already turning their thoughts to the great Himalaya. The brothers Schlagintweit climbed to 22,260 feet on Kamet. Officers of the Survey of India, in the course of their duties, were brought among the great peaks and in their records are statements that J. S. Pocock climbed to 22,000 feet in Garhwal in 1874, and that W. Johnson climbed a peak in the Kuen Lun whose altitude was afterwards determined as 23,890 feet.

The main attack on the great peaks has, however, been made by men from Europe trained in the technique of mountain craft which has gradually developed in Alpine climbing. They came from nearly every European country, as well as from America. Graham, in 1883, claims to have reached an altitude of 23,185 feet. Sir Martin Conway pioneered the way among the Karakoram giants of the Baltoro Glacier. The Swiss, Dr Jacot Guillarmod, explored in the same region. The Americans, Dr and Mrs Bullock Workman, attained a height of 23,400 feet. Dr Longstaff reached the summit of Trisul, 23,406 feet. Douglas Freshfield explored Kangchenjunga.

Then came the most serious and best organized effort to ascertain to what altitude it was possible for man to ascend on a mountain. For it is not the physical obstacle which a mountain presents – rocky precipices or snow and ice – that stands in the way of man's reaching the highest summits of the Himalaya. In the Alps, where the actual climbing is just as hard as any in the Himalaya, man has been able to overcome every obstacle of that kind. He ascends the most appalling precipices and crags and finds his way up the most forbidding ice cliffs. Nor is the cold of the Himalaya the deterrent: man has withstood much severer cold in the polar regions. The real obstacle is the want of oxygen in the air at high altitudes. The air grows thinner and thinner the higher we ascend. And as it grows thinner the less oxygen in it is there. And oxygen is one of the substances on which man depends for his minute by minute bodily sustenance. The question, then, which the Italian expedition under the Duke of the Abruzzi came out to determine, was to what height in this thin air, so deficient in oxygen, man could ascend on a mountain side by his own unaided efforts. This was in 1919, and owing to the difficulty at that time in obtaining permission from either the government of Nepal or Tibet, between which countries Mount Everest is situated, it was not possible for the Duke to make his experiment on that mountain. He selected therefore the next highest, namely K2, in the Karakoram Himalaya, which is 28,278 feet in height. And this peak proving an impractical mountain he climbed another, Bride Peak, to an altitude of 24,600 feet and would certainly have reached higher but for the mist and snowstorms.

Man was thus steadily marching to dominion over the mountain, and already the idea of climbing Mount Everest itself had been forming itself in his mind. As far back as 1893, Captain (now Brigadier General) Hon C. G. Bruce had thought of it. He had been with Sir Martin Conway in the Karakoram Himalaya and when employed in Chitral suggested the idea. But the opportunity for carrying it out never occurred. Many years later Lord Curzon, when Viceroy of India, made a proposal to Mr Douglas Freshfield that the Royal Geographical Society and the Alpine Club should join in organizing an expedition to Mount Everest, if he, Lord Curzon, could obtain permission from the Nepal government to send the expedition through Nepal. This permission, however, was not forthcoming, so nothing came of Lord Curzon's proposal. The Nepalese are a very seclusive people, but as they have been for many years friendly to the British the government of India humour them in their desire to be left to themselves.

When Mr Freshfield, who had already been President of the Alpine Club, became President of the Royal Geographical Society, he undoubtedly would have taken up an idea so congenial to him as organizing a Mount Everest expedition. But it so happened that his period of office fell during the war. After the war the idea was revived by Captain Noel, who had made a reconnaissance into Tibet in the direction of the mountain in 1913 at a time when the late Brig General Rawling was also cherishing the hope of at least reconnoitring Everest. And when the present writer became President of the Royal Geographical Society in 1920 the time seemed ripe for bringing the idea of climbing Mount Everest into effect. He had spent many years in the Himalaya and had been in Tibet itself. He therefore knew the local conditions. And with the resources of a big society much could be done that was difficult for single individuals, or for small parties of three or four, like those which climb in the Alps.

Meanwhile, there had been a great development in another direction. Actually while the Duke was climbing in the Himalaya, Bleriot was flying across the Channel. And the Great War gave a tremendous impetus to aeroplane construction. As a result men were now able to fly higher even than the top of Mount Everest. The question how high men could ascend seemed therefore to be a matter more for the airman than the mountaineer; and the former had already beaten the latter. Why then take the trouble to climb Mount Everest which would prove nothing but what had already been proved?

The reply is that the two problems differ entirely. The airman sits in his machine and sucks oxygen and the machine carries him upward. He needs skill and nerve of course to fly the machine properly. Still, he is carried up by the machine. He does not carry himself up. And he can have plenty of oxygen beside him to make up for the deficiency in the atmosphere. The climber has to rise on his own steam. He has to keep to the earth's surface. And what we want to know is if there is any part of the earth's surface so high that he cannot by his own unaided effort reach it. So we select the highest mountain and make our experiment on that.

Some people indeed do ask what all this pother is about. If you want to get to the top of Mount Everest why not get an aeroplane to dump you down there? A similar question might be asked of a university crew. If they want to get from Putney to Mortlake why not go in a motor boat: they would reach there much quicker and more comfortably than by rowing themselves there in a boat. Or the runner in a mile race might be asked why he did not call a taxicab.

Man means to *climb* Mount Everest – climb it on his own feet. That is the whole point. Only so does he get that pride in his prowess which is such a satisfaction to his soul. Life would be a poor affair if we relied always on the machine. We are too prone already to trust to science and mechanics instead of exerting our own bodies and our own spirit. And we thereby miss much of that enjoyment in life which exercising our faculties to the full brings with it.

And so we come back to the point from which we started. This determination to climb Mount Everest has grown out of the ordinary impulse men have to climb the hill in their neighbourhood. In the case of Mount Everest a mightier effort is required, but the impulse to make it is of the same origin. Indeed, the struggle with Everest is all part and parcel of the perpetual struggle of spirit to establish its supremacy over matter. Man, the spiritual, means to make himself supreme over even the mightiest of what is material.

Both man and mountain have emerged from the same original earth and therefore have something in common between them. But the mountain is the lower in the scale of being, however massive and impressive in outward appearance. And man, the punier in appearance but the greater in reality, has that within him which will not let him rest until he has planted his foot on the topmost summit of the highest embodiment of the lower. He will not be daunted by bulk. The mountain may be high. But he will show that his spirit is higher. And he will not be content until he has it in subjection under his feet.

This is the secret in the heart of the idea of climbing Mount Everest.

And in proving his powers man would find that joy which their exercise ever gives.

Chapter Two

PREPARATION

The idea of climbing Mount Everest had thus entered into men's minds and was slowly spreading there and penetrating deeper. Men were no longer content with idly contemplating the mountain from a distance. They must be up and grappling with it. The time for action had arrived. And how the idea was put into execution is the story now to be told. It necessarily divides itself into three phases. First there is the phase when the mountain had to be prospected carefully; for no one yet – no European – had been within forty miles of it. This was the reconnaissance phase. Then, a practical way up having been discovered by Mallory, came the actual attempt to reach the summit – an attempt which did not succeed – but which showed that men could climb to 27,000 feet. Lastly, came the second attempt which ended so tragically, but in which men, with no adventitious aid, climbed to 28,100 feet.

These are the three phases of the high adventure; and it is with the first that we will now deal.

Before any great idea can be put into execution there are usually a number of preliminary barriers which have to be removed. In this case the first barriers were human. The

Nepalese barred the way to Mount Everest from the south. The Tibetans had hitherto barred it on the north. Could the reluctance of the latter to admit strangers be overcome? That was the first matter to be tackled. It was a question of diplomacy and that art had to be exercised before an expedition could be launched.

A deputation composed of members of the Royal Geographical Society and the Alpine Club waited on the Secretary of State for India to acquaint him with the import-ance which the two bodies attached to the project and to enlist his sympathy. Should that sympathy be forthcoming, and he have no objection to an Everest expedition being sent to Tibet, provided the sanction of the government of India and the Tibetan government were obtained, the two societies proposed inviting Colonel Howard Bury to proceed to India to negotiate the matter with the government of India. This was the representation that was made to him.

By a strange coincidence the deputation (which was headed by the President of the Royal Geographical Society) was received by Lord Sinha, who was then Under-Secretary of State. He was a Bengali, from whose native province Mount Everest can be seen. Perhaps he himself was not particularly enthusiastic about the scheme. But speaking as the mouthpiece of the Secretary of State he said that no objection would be raised by the India Office.

This was one barrier out of the way. And it might have been insuperable. For a previous Secretary of State *had* raised objections to Englishmen travelling in Tibet. He held the view that travellers caused trouble and should be discouraged.

To remove the next barrier Colonel Howard Bury was

dispatched to India. He was an officer of the 60th Rifles who, after service in the Great War, had just retired. Before the war he had served in India and been on shooting expeditions in the Himalaya. And being interested in the Everest project put himself at the disposal of the Royal Geographical Society. He proved an excellent ambassador. He inspired Lord Chelmsford, the Viceroy, and Lord Rawlinson, the Commander-in-Chief, with enthusiasm for the idea, and he got a promise of their support if the local agent, Mr Bell, should think the Tibetans would raise no objection. Colonel Howard Bury then proceeded to Sikkim and saw Mr Bell and got him also interested. And, fortunately, Mr (now Sir Charles) Bell had great influence with the Tibetans. The result was that by the end of 1920 news came to London that the Tibetan government had granted permission for an expedition to proceed to Mount Everest in the following year.

Diplomacy having achieved its object and human obstacles being overcome it was possible to go full steam ahead organizing an expedition. And climbing Mount Everest was a matter which interested both the Royal Geographical Society and the Alpine Club. It interested the former because the society will not admit that there is any spot on the earth's surface on which man should not at least try to set his foot. And it interested the latter because climbing mountains is their especial province. It was decided, therefore, to make the expedition a joint effort of the two societies. And this was the more desirable because the Geographical Society had greater facilities for organizing exploring expeditions, while the Alpine Club had better means of choosing the personnel. A joint committee, called the Mount Everest Committee, was therefore formed, composed of three members each of the two societies. And it was arranged that during the first phase, while the mountain was being reconnoitred, the President of the Royal Geographical Society should be Chairman; and in the second phase, when the mountain was to be climbed, the President of the Alpine Club should preside.

Thus constituted, the Mount Everest Committee was composed of the following:

Sir Francis Younghusband (Chairman) Mr Edward Somers-Cocks Colonel Jacks	Representing the Royal Geographical Society
Professor Norman Collie (President, Alpine Club) Captain J. P. Farrar (Ex-president, Alpine Club) Mr. C. F. Meade	Representing the Alpine Club

Mr Eaton and Mr Hinks were Honorary Secretaries.

As ever, the first necessity was money – and Everest expeditions are expensive matters. Neither of the two societies had any money at their disposal; so all had to be raised by private subscription. And here the Alpine Club were extraordinarily generous – or anyhow they were made to be by the compelling Captain Farrar. If a single member had a single sovereign to spare Farrar forced him to disgorge it. In the Geographical Society there still lingered the notion that climbing Mount Everest was sensational but not 'scientific'. If it were a matter of making a *map* of the region, then the project should be encouraged. If it were a question merely of climbing the mountain, then it should be left to mountaineers and not absorb the attention of a scientific body like the Royal Geographical Society.

This narrow view of the functions of the society was strongly held by some fellows – even by an ex-President. It was a survival of times when the making of a map was looked upon as the be-all and end-all of a geographer. But it was now laid down from the very first that the attainment of the summit of Mount Everest was the supreme object of the expedition and all other objects subsidiary to that. Climbing the mountain was no mere sensationalism. It was testing the capacity of man. If he could pass the test of climbing the highest mountain, he would feel himself capable of climbing every other peak that did not present insuperable physical obstacles; and the range of geographers would be extended into new and unexplored regions of the earth.

As to the map: that would follow right enough. Let it be known that we were out on a great adventure, and map-makers, geologists, naturalists, botanists and all the rest would come flocking in. That was the view put before the society and which the society adopted.

Concurrently with collecting the money, the Mount Everest Committee concerned itself with collecting the men and purchasing the equipment and stores. And the composition of the party was determined by the primary object with which the first expedition would be dispatched; and that object was reconnaissance. For it must be explained that up till now little was known of the mountain itself. Its position and height had been determined by observations made from stations in the plains of India more than a hundred miles away. But from the plains only the tip of it can be seen. A little more can be seen from the neighbourhood of Darjiling, but even then only at a distance of eighty miles. From the Tibetan side Rawling and Ryder had approached to within about sixty miles and Noel perhaps closer. Still, all this did not tell us very much about the mountain. The upper portion looked reasonably practicable. But what it was like between 16,000 feet and 26,000 feet, no one could say.

Douglas Freshfield and Norman Collie, who had both climbed in the Himalaya and who both had a keen eye for mountain topography, were, therefore, strongly of opinion that a whole season should be devoted to a thorough reconnaissance of the mountain so that not only *a* route to the summit but also that route which would indubitably be the best should be found. For it was certain that it would only be by the easiest way up that the summit would ever be reached. And it would be disastrous if a party, after toiling up one route and failing to attain its object, were afterwards to find that a better route was all the time available.

Reconnaissance being the object of the first expedition, it was necessary to choose a man to lead the climbers who was a good judge of a mountain – a man of wide experience in mountaineering, who would be able to give an authoritative opinion on the vital question of the route. Mr Harold Raeburn had this experience and he had, as it happened, on the previous year been climbing in Sikkim. He was somewhat old, but he would not be expected to climb to any great heights and it was hoped that his experience would compensate for his age.

For the higher climbing that might be necessary, and for the real attempt which would be made on the following year, one name was immediately mentioned by the Alpine Club members, and that name was Mallory. There was no question in their mind that he was the finest climber they had. George Leigh Mallory was then a master at Charterhouse. There was nothing remarkable in his appearance. He was of the ordinary type of young man that you see in thousands every day. He was not like Bruce was at the same age, a giant of strength and bursting with physical energy. Nor was he of the wiry, vivid, alert type we see among Frenchmen and Italians. He was certainly good-looking, with a sensitive, cultivated air. And now and then he would speak in a sudden, perhaps rather jerky, impatient way, showing that there was more going on within him than met the eye. But no one who had not seen him on a mountain would have remarked anything very special in him. And if the man in the street had had the selection of the climbers he would have chosen robuster, more vigorous-looking men than Mallory.

Nor did Mallory give the appearance of bursting himself with enthusiasm to join the expedition. When the committee had made their choice he was asked by Farrar to meet the Chairman at luncheon. The situation was to be discussed and the Chairman was to make him the definite invitation to join. But when the invitation was made he accepted it without visible emotion. He had the self-confidence of assured position as a climber. He had neither exaggerated modesty nor pushful self-assertiveness. He was conscious of his own powers and of the position he had won by his own exertions; and he had, in consequence, a not obtrusive but quite perceptible and quite justifiable pride in himself as a mountaineer.

Only one indication was there of the fire that all the time was burning within. A question had arisen about the inclusion of a certain other climber in the party. As a mountaineer this other was all that could be desired; but he had characteristics which several members of the committee who knew him thought would cause friction and irritation in the party and destroy that cohesion which is so vitally necessary in an Everest expedition. At high altitudes it is well known that men become irritable. And at the altitudes of Mount Everest they might find it wholly impossible to contain their irritation; and an uncongenial member might break up the party. It was an urgent matter; and to put it further to the test the Chairman consulted Mallory and asked him whether he would be prepared to sleep in the same bag with this man at 27,000 feet. Mallory, in that quick, sudden way he used when he was intent on a thing, said that he 'didn't care who he slept with as long as they got to the top.'

From the manner in which he said this there was no question of his keenness. And, if he was not of the conventional bulldog, heavy-jawed, determined type; and, if he was not boisterously enthusiastic, he was evidently keen enough at bottom – keener than the most boisterous.

He was then a man of thirty-three, slim and supple if not broad and beefy. He was a Winchester boy and had, while still at school, been inspired with the love of mountaineering by that well-known mountain-loving master, Mr Irving. He had responded from the first, and was now both an ardent and a skilful mountaineer.

George Finch was the next choice. He had the reputation of being a most competent and determined mountaineer. And his keenness was evident from the first moment. When the committee had decided upon selecting him he was asked to come and see the Chairman. The Chairman then made to him the formal invitation. For a few seconds he seemed unable to speak from the intensity of emotion that was surging within him. Then he said, 'Sir Francis, you've sent me to heaven.' He was a tall, well-made athletic man with a determined look about him. But clearly he was not in good health. And when he went to the doctor – as all members of the expedition had to – he was turned down. And a bitter pill it was for him to swallow – though in the following year he was able to join the next expedition.

A substitute had hastily to be found and Mallory suggested his old schoolfellow and mountaineering companion, Mr Bullock, then (and now) in the Consular Service, but at home on leave. A reference to Lord Curzon, then Foreign Secretary, at once produced the required extension of leave and Bullock joined the expedition. He was much more of the build the inexperienced would expect of an Everest climber; squarer and stronger than either Mallory or Finch; and at school he had been a long-distance runner and had great staying power. One further qualification he had: a placid temperament and the ability to sleep under any conditions.

As naturalist and medical officer an excellent man was available – A. F. R. Wollaston. He had already made a reputation as an explorer in New Guinea, Ruwenzori, and elsewhere. He was also a good mountaineer, a keen naturalist, a cheery companion, and a man who could deal sympathetically with natives.

Others who would join the expedition in India were Dr

Kellas, and the surveyor officers, Major H. T. Morshead, DSO, and Captain E. O. Wheeler, MC.

Kellas had made many expeditions in Sikkim and other parts of the Himalaya. He was a lecturer in chemistry who had for years made a study of the use of oxygen for climbing at high altitudes. And he was one of those indefatigable men who cannot be torn away from their special pursuits. In the previous summer he had made an ascent to 23,000 feet and should during the cold weather have taken a rest. But he spent all the time climbing in Sikkim, living on very poor and insufficient food.

Morshead was known for his exploration, with Major F. M. Bailey, of the course of the Tsang-po, or Brahmaputra, as it cut through the Himalaya; and both he and Wheeler were eminently competent to make the required map of Mount Everest and its surroundings; though Morshead had not the training in the technique of climbing or the experience of snow and ice which were so necessary for the actual climbers.

This was the party, and as leader of it Colonel C. K. Howard Bury was selected. He was only a 'walker': he was not a 'climber' in the Alpine Club sense. But he had done a good deal of shooting, both in the Alps and the Himalaya, and, what was more necessary for the leader, he knew how to deal with Asiatics, and could be trusted to lead the expedition without friction through Tibet.

While the party was being formed, numerous applications were received for inclusion in it. Men from nearly all over the world wrote saying that they were ready to go in any capacity. Many of these applications were curious productions, setting forth the candidate's claims and limitations in the most appealing fashion. A particularly quaint one which reached the Chairman he put before the committee as perhaps about 'the limit', and it caused much merriment, until his daughter asked him to observe the date. It had arrived on April 1st! Except this the others were undoubtedly genuine – and testified to the keenness for adventure there is in men. They also brought out in glaring relief the value of training and experience. Every single one had to be turned down when such men as Mallory and Finch were available. The untrained and inexperienced, however keen, had not a ghost of a chance beside proved mountaineers.

The collection of money and the selection of men had to be supplemented by the purchase of supplies and equipment and instruments. Farrar and Meade dealt with supplies and equipment: Jacks and Hinks with instruments.

If Farrar had not been on the wrong side of sixty he would have been the very man to get to the top of Everest. Of marvellous energy, full of pluck and go, of wide and long experience and of that combination of care and daring which is essential for great enterprise, he would indeed have put Everest on her mettle. As he could not go with the expedition he concentrated his energy on collecting money and efficiently equipping it. And in this he was assisted by Meade, who the year before had climbed to 23,000 feet in the Himalaya and knew the requirements.

Jacks, who was the Chief of the Geographical Section of the War Office, and Hinks, the Secretary of the Royal Geographical Society, were of course peculiarly well fitted to choose the cameras, theodolite, compasses, etc., which were required, and to look after all geographical requirements.

The committee were always able to have the best advice on any line. For the aim being to attain the highest, and nothing but the best, whether in men or material, being good enough for that purpose, the best men in every line were interested in the adventure. And among them Dr De Filippi, the very capable and experienced Italian explorer and scientist, who had accompanied the Duke of the Abruzzi.

None were more interested than Their Majesties the King and Queen, and HRH The Prince of Wales.

The expedition started, therefore, the best manned and equipped expedition which had ever tackled the Himalaya, and with the good wishes of the highest in the land.

Chapter Three

THE START

Mallory actually leaving for Everest was a different man from
Mallory somewhat impassively receiving the invitation. The
joy of great struggle was clearly arising. Friends were wishing
him 'Good Luck' and wanted to be with him. The life and stir
of great action were beginning to thrill. And then there was the
possibility – the bare possibility – being whispered about that
perhaps that very summer he might conquer Mount Everest.
Who knows? The ascent might be easier than expected. All
that could be seen *looked* easy. And if the mountain sides below
that could be seen proved easy too, why – he might reach the
top this same season. The instructions did not *preclude* an
attempt. The reconnaissance was insisted on as the primary
object of the year's expedition. And the climbers were not to
make an attempt on a difficult route on the mere chance of
reaching the summit: they were to go on and look for a better.
But if they actually found a quite feasible route to the summit,
why then, of course, they were not to be prevented from having
a try.

This was one of those vague hopes with which members and
leaders and organizers of expeditions buoy themselves up when

they have made every preparation and discounted every danger, hardship and physical obstacle. Men's hopes ever do stretch beyond the actual limits of their task. Though they like also that their performance should outstrip their promise. Therefore they do not publish their hopes for the multitude to scoff at. Their secret hopes they keep to themselves.

It is a far cry from London to Mount Everest (4000 miles as the crow flies). But Everest climbers are not crows – not even airmen. They had accordingly to proceed across France, down the Mediterranean Sea, down the Red Sea, across the Indian Ocean, and then across India from Bombay to Calcutta and finally to Darjiling, the assembling place of the expedition.

Raeburn had preceded Mallory to Darjiling to collect the porters, and Howard Bury, Bullock and Wollaston were proceeding thither by different routes.

Porters for the service of the expedition were to be enlisted. And this engagement of selected porters was a special feature of the expedition. It was the result of a recommendation by General Bruce. Hitherto, expeditions to the Himalaya had been dependent on the inhabitants of the highest villages for the carriage of their stores and equipment. Men were caught up from these villages and induced to carry loads. Sometimes this was satisfactory. Sometimes it was not. For quite small climbs it answered. But for expeditions of the size of an Everest expedition it was impracticable. Moreover, in this case the climbers would have to depend on Tibetan villagers, and it might not be possible to induce even a few Tibetans to hazard the hardships and dangers of climbing on Mount Everest.

General Bruce's idea was, then, to take measures well beforehand to get together fit and willing men from the neighbourhood of Darjiling, and from these to select about forty of the best. These forty would then be formed into a corps. They would be infused with an *esprit de corps*. Appeal would be made to their spirit of adventure, their love of fame and honour, their ambition to make a name for themselves. And they would be paid well, fed well, equipped well – and also ruled well, so that by the childish indulgences to which they are prone they would not risk the success of the expedition.

In this part of the Himalaya there are plenty of hardy, cheery men, not very venturesome on their own initiative, but ready enough to join in an adventure when some one would lead them. Among the Sherpas of Eastern Nepal are many such. And there are Bhotias from round Darjiling and Tibetans settled in Sikkim. From amongst all these it would be possible to raise a most efficient corps. And they would all be men who from their youth had been accustomed to carrying loads – and carrying them at high altitudes, some of them as high as 18,000 or 19,000 feet.

Here at Darjiling, early in May, porters, climbers, stores and equipment of all kinds were gradually assembled and local stores, such as tea, sugar, flour and potatoes were purchased. And the climbers were entertained and the expedition given every assistance by Lord Ronaldshay, then Governor of Bengal.

For natural beauty Darjiling is surely unsurpassed in the world. From all countries travellers come there to see the famous view of Kangchenjunga, 28,150 feet in height, and only forty miles distant. Darjiling itself is 7000 feet above sea level and is set in a forest of oaks, magnolia, rhododendrons, laurels and sycamores. And through these forests the observer looks down the steep mountain sides to the Rangeet River only 1000 feet above sea level, and then up and up through tier after tier of forest-clad ranges, each bathed in a haze of deeper and deeper purple, till the line of snow is reached; and then still up to the summit of Kangchenjunga, now so pure and ethereal we can scarcely believe it is part of the solid earth on which we stand; and so high it seems part of the very sky itself.

And yet these Everest climbers were aspiring after something higher still. Kangchenjunga was but the third highest mountain. So it they spurned. 'Only the highest', was their motto.

By the middle of May Howard Bury had collected his whole party and their equipment and stores. Dr A. M. Kellas had come in from his winter tour in Sikkim, but very much the worse for it. In the early spring he had spent several nights on the slopes of Kabru with very low temperatures. And he was not a man who looked after himself: he subsisted mainly on what the country could produce, and this particular country did not produce very wholesome or nutritious food. Consequently, he arrived at Darjiling in very poor condition. And this only just before the expedition started, so he had no time to recuperate. The two survey officers, Morshead and Wheeler, deputed by the government of India to make the survey, had also arrived. They were both strong, hardy men accustomed to ascending the minor peaks of the Himalaya, and Wheeler had climbed in Canada; he was an expert in the Canadian system of photo survey and was prepared to use it on this expedition. Dr A. M. Heron, of the Geological Survey of India, also joined the expedition. And these with the members from England made up the party.

But the expedition could not proceed from Darjiling direct to Everest; they had to make a long detour. The direct route would have been westward through Nepal; the expedition had to go eastward through Tibet because Nepal was forbidden land.

Howard Bury and his party made, therefore, for the Tista Valley of Sikkim, out of which they would climb up to the Jelap La, following the main trade route to Lhasa for some marches – not a high road for carts, but a rough road for mules. They would pass through wonderful forests at first and then have to march for 200 miles over the lofty arid plateau of Tibet. But they would reap this advantage, that they would at the end be halfway up the mountain, for the plateau of Tibet is about 15,000 feet high. And through being at that height for some weeks they would have been acclimatizing themselves for attaining higher heights.

They started from Darjiling on May 18th. The night before the rain had come down in torrents – as is its wont in Darjiling for a great number of days in the year: such glories as the view of Kangchenjunga must always be paid for. The rain held up soon after the expedition started, but the mountain sides were wreathed in soft grey mists and every moss-hung branch and tree dripped with moisture all day long. This indeed was unpleasant, yet this dripping forest had a beauty of its own. Every growth was fresh. The green was brilliant. And the ferns and orchids, the hanging mosses and long-trailing creepers were ever-varying delights.

Tea gardens, useful maybe, but, in their regular rows of low green bushes, not beautiful like the forest round them, were passed on the way. And now the path began to descend from the ridge; the air became hotter and hotter; men and beasts were bathed in perspiration; the vegetation changed with the climate; tree ferns twenty to thirty feet in height, wild bananas, and palms appeared; and most glorious of all, numbers of gorgeous butterflies.

When the Tista River was reached the expedition was, in fact, in a tropical climate, for the river is only 700 feet above sea level and the latitude is only 26 degrees. The heat was intense and in this confined valley, with a moist atmosphere and seldom any wind, the vegetation is that of a tropical forest. And what constitutes one of the glories of this valley is that it extends upwards to the very glaciers of Kangchenjunga, so that plant and animal life from tropical to arctic are herein found.

At Kalimpong, which is about 3000 feet above the Tista, they were entertained by the well-known Dr Graham, and found a beautiful garden filled with roses and scarlet hibiscus and a large-flowered mauve solanum growing up the pillars of the verandahs.

At Pedong, Howard Bury notes great trees of scarlet hibiscus, daturas and bougainvillaeas. And wonderful datura hedges, with trees fifteen to twenty feet in height, laden with hundreds of white trumpet-shaped blooms eight inches in diameter and fully a foot long were seen. At night these great white flowers glowed as though with phosphorescence and they had a strangely sweet smell. There were also orchids of the Dendrobium, Coelogene, and Cymbidium families, mauve, white and yellow – some with sprays eighteen inches long.

The flowers and the butterflies were a wonder. But the weather was dreadful. Rain fell in sheets. And no waterproof was proof against it. Every one was soaked. And the constant rain had brought out the leeches waiting in their myriads on leaf and branch to attach themselves to man or animal.

At Rongli, where they halted on May 22nd, caladiums, kolocasias and begonias were growing on every rock, and the stems of many of the trees were decorated with the large shiny leaves of the giant pothos. Other climbers, vine and peppers and the like, were suspended from tree to tree. The branches were frequently matted thick with orchids. And the trees themselves were often fully 150 feet in height, some with clean straight trunks for a 100 feet without a branch.

But from Rongli they climbed steeply out of the tropical forest into the zone of flowering rhododendrons. The first met with in the upward road were the *R. argenteum* and *R. falconeri* growing in a great forest of oaks and magnolias covered with delicate ferns and mauve or white orchids. Higher up the path were masses of *R. cinnabarinum*, whose flowers displayed every shade of red and orange. Higher still came rhododendrons of every colour – pink, crimson, yellow, mauve, white and cream.

Among the smaller flowers was a large pink saxifrage; and a deep reddish purple primula covered every open space. Other primulas were a very tiny pink one and another like a pink primrose.

To flower-lovers, like Howard Bury, Mallory and Wollaston, these were a perpetual delight. They were all the more appreciated because they would be almost the last sign of luxuriance and grace they would behold before they had to face the austerities and stern realities of rock and ice and snow, and the frosts of Mount Everest.

Chapter Four

CHUMBI

The Chumbi Valley which the expedition would now be entering has not the wealth of tree and plant life that Sikkim has. Nor has it the same views of stupendous snowy ranges rising right out of the forests. Chumbi is built on a smaller scale, but it is a more agreeable valley to travel through. The rainfall is less by two-thirds. The air is more bracing and the sunshine more certain. Except that in Kashmir there are no rhododendrons it is very like a Kashmir valley. Mountains of the Alpine order of magnitude rise from the valley bottom, and the river, though rapid and sparkling, is not of the raging, tearing, omnipotent description that the Tista is. An account of the chief flowers and trees met with on the way is as good a means as any of conveying an idea of what the valley is like.

From the rhododendron zone in Sikkim the expedition climbed, in pouring rain, to the Jelep Pass, 14,390 feet, and from there looked down into Tibetan territory – though not into what is geographically Tibet, for they were not yet over the main watershed but were looking into the Chumbi Valley, which is on the Indian side.

Crossing the pass made a change in climate. They emerged

from the mist and rain and were under the clean blue sky which is one characteristic of Tibet. And they were entering the Chumbi Valley when it was at its best. As they rapidly descended the zigzag path they were once again among rhododendrons and primulas. Nearing the 12,000-feet level, Wollaston noticed the open level spaces were carpeted with a dark purple and yellow primula (*P. gammiena*), a delicate little yellow flower (*Lloydia tibetica*) and many saxifrages, while the steep hill sides were ablaze with the flowers of the large rhododendrons (*R. thomsoni, R. falconeri, R. aucklandi*) and the smaller campylocarpum, in great variety of colour. The descent continued through woods of pines, oaks and walnuts. And lower down were a fine white clematis, a pink and white spiraea, a yellow berberis and white roses, while a dark purple iris grew in profusion.

Yatung, where there is a British Trade Agent and a guard of twenty-five Indian troops, was reached on the same day. It lies at a height of 9400 feet. Apples and pears do well there. Wheat and potatoes are grown in great quantities. And in May the air was scented by the wild roses which grow in large bushes covered with hundreds of cream-coloured blossoms.

On May 27th the expedition began its ascent of the main Chumbi Valley towards Phari and the plateau of Tibet proper. The path lay close beside the clear rushing river. More wild roses, including a large red one, pink and white spiraeas and cotoneasters, anemones, berberis, clematis and some charming dwarf rhododendrons abounded. And as they neared the Lingmatang Plain there were masses of pink and mauve rhododendrons, flowering cherries, viburnum, berberis and roses. The plain itself is about 11,000 feet above sea level, and is a lovely meadow, covered now with a tiny pink primula (*P. minutissima*).

Beyond the plain the path ascended again through forests of birch, larch, juniper, spruce, and silver fir, with an undergrowth of rhododendrons and mountain ash. Blue poppies, fritillaries, ground orchids and sweet-scented primulas grew along the path. And in the forest were great bushes, eight to ten feet in height, of *R. cinnabarinum* which is here at its best and varied in shade from yellow and orange to deep red.

Dippers, wagtails and the white-capped redstart were the commonest birds along the river-banks. In the woods hereabouts the blood pheasant was often heard, and sometimes seen. Here lives also, though it was not to be seen, the great Tibetan stag which in size nearly rivals the wapiti.

Above Gautsa, 12,000 feet, both the vegetation and the country began to change. The rhododendrons were still the most beautiful of the flowering shrubs but were diminished in size. Howard Bury speaks of a pale blue iris. And Wollaston marked especially a yellow primula covering the ground more thickly than cowslips in England and filling the air with its scent. Here and there was seen the large blue poppy (*Meconopsis sp.*), some of whose flowers were fully three inches across; and a white anemone with five or six flowers on one stem.

Soon the trees became scantier, pines disappeared altogether; birches, willows and junipers followed. Dwarf rhododendrons, only a foot high, some pure white, others pink, continued up to about 13,500 feet. And then the hill sides became purple with the little *rhododendron setosum*, which covered the hill sides like purple heather.

After eight miles the country changed completely in

character. The gorges and deep, richly-wooded valleys were left behind. And the expedition came out on to the open plain of Phari – the real Tibet, though the actual watershed was yet a few miles further on. And there, standing sentinel over the entrance to Tibet, was the great peak Chomolhari, 23,930 feet in height – not one of the highest peaks, but one of the most conspicuous and beautiful peaks, because it stands so apart from the rest and is so sharp and bold and rugged in its outline.

Chapter Five

TIBET

The holiday part of the expedition was now over and business was to commence. But the members of the expedition on their arrival in Tibet were in no fit state for the hard work before them. The great contrast of climate they had experienced since leaving England, the alternate heat and cold, dry heat and steaming heat, dry cold and wet cold, the changes of diet, and perhaps also bad and filthy cooking had knocked up nearly every one. Kellas was the worst, and as soon as he arrived in Phari he retired to bed.

The weather, now they had arrived in Tibet, was, however, at least healthy. The soaking mists, the drenching rains and the enervating heat were finally left behind. The billowy monsoon clouds did not reach Tibet. The sky was clear and the air was dry even if there were too much of it at times.

Phari was a filthy place, as every traveller, from the time of Manning in 1811 on, has irresistibly remarked. It is a fort surrounded by a little town set out in the plain. But the Dzongpen – the local official – was civil and helpful. Tibetans are by nature courteous. They may be obstinate and, if aroused by anything which touches their religion, they may vehemently hate. But their native disposition is polite. And in this case the Dzongpen had received orders from Lhasa to provide the required transport – on payment – and to be friendly with the British.

Transport therefore was forthcoming, though it took time to collect, and the expedition spent several days at Phari.

From this dirty place they marched across the Tang La, 15,200 feet, to Tuna. The rise is scarcely perceptible and the pass itself is a plain two or three miles wide. For these reasons the pass has great importance. It forms the main approach to Tibet from India and is the way by which the Tibet Mission of 1904 proceeded to Lhasa. They were able to cross it even in the depth of winter – January the 9th – though the thermometer fell to 18 degrees below zero at night, and during the day a violent bitter wind was blowing. On the far side there is scarcely any descent, and Tuna, where the Tibet Mission spent the months of January, February and March, is 15,000 feet above sea level.

The high lands of Tibet had now been reached. For hundreds of miles, to the borders of China on the east and Chinese Turkestan on the north, they consist of wide open plains at an altitude of between 14,000 and 15,000 feet, bounded by bare rounded ranges of hills, rising a few thousand feet above them and breaking into rugged crags near the summits and capped with snow and ice when an altitude of 20,000 or more is attained. This is the general character of Tibet. Under some aspects it is bare and desolate and repellent. And the incessant, tearing winds chill both the spirit and the body. But Tibet has at least one good trait: the early mornings are usually calm. The sky is then of transparent, purest azure. The sun is warm.

The snowy summits of some distant peaks are tinged with delicate pinks and primrose. And the heart of man warms even to Tibet.

That Tibet is a high plateau of this description is due to lack of rain. Rain falls in a deluge on the Indian side of the Himalaya, but little passes over the range into Tibet. As a consequence, the plateau has not been scoured out into deep valleys such as are found on the Indian side. And this want of rain means also sparseness of plant life; and paucity of plants means that animals are few. Its want of vegetation means also that the barren rocks and soil heat up under the sun and chill rapidly at night and so we find Tibet a land of furious winds.

A blue sky, constant sunshine, fierce winds, extremes of temperature, severe cold, a barren landscape – these are the features of Tibet; and the altitude gives to the European a constant sense of being only half his real self.

Under these conditions it is not surprising that plant life is almost imperceptible. You look out over those open plains and all appears like a desert. You cannot imagine how living things could subsist there. And yet you do see flocks of sheep and herds of yak. And as you observe more closely you do see scrub of some kind – a blade of grass here and another there – and in the summer even flowers: a little trumpet-shaped purple incarvillea, and a dwarf blue iris are common. And in winter the animals shuffle the surface and get at the roots of plants to subsist on them. Sheep are worn down to the bare bone, and a leg of mutton in winter affords only one helping at meals. Yet somehow they survive, in spite of the cold, of the winds, and of the scarcity of food, till the quick short summer season arrives when grass rapidly springs up.

Besides the domestic animals there is more wildlife than one would suppose. Among the most common animals are mouse-hares or pikas, delightful little creatures about the size of a guinea pig, quick and lively in their movements and darting from hole to hole with extreme rapidity. They live in colonies on the less stony part of the plain, or on grassy patches, when they can find them, and form burrows in which they store up quantities of seed during the summer, and hibernate in the winter. The Tibetan hare lives among the heaps of debris which accumulate at the foot of the hills. On the hills themselves the wild sheep, burrhel and *ovis hodgsoni* are found. The graceful little gazelle is often seen on the open plateau, and occasionally, in small parties, the kiang or wild ass. Wolves also there are and foxes, though they are not often seen. And, whether it is as a protection against beasts and birds of prey, or from some other reason, these animals are as a rule of some shade of buff or brown which resembles the plateau soil.

And this protective coloration is the more noticeable in bird life. Larks, wheatears and mountain finches are the commonest birds. The Tibetan skylark is almost identical with our own and its song may be heard over every patch of native cultivation. Five kinds of mountain finch were seen by Hingston, the naturalist of the third expedition. They were all fairly well protected by the colour of their plumage, which was of some shade of brown or fulvous, dull and inconspicuous. Sand grouse of a pale fawn plumage which blends with the open ground live on the open stony plain and congregate in considerable flocks. On the slopes of the hills partridges are found, and in the ravines Alpine choughs, rock doves and crag martins. In and around the villages are sparrows and robins. Wollaston also saw a cuckoo on a telegraph wire.

The 'enemy' in this bird and animal life is represented by wolves and foxes on the ground, and by eagles, buzzards and kestrels in the air. It is against these that birds and animals have to protect themselves by coloration. And the great lammergeier vultures are ever circling overhead on the look-out for any kill.

But among the 'enemy' man is not to be reckoned. The Tibetans cannot be said never to take life, for meat is to be had in Tibet. But, in principle, they are against taking life and the wild animals are not hunted. Indeed, around some of the monasteries they are actually fed and have become so tame that wild sheep would come close up to the camp of the expedition. This respect for animal life is inculcated by the Buddhist religion which the Tibetans profess. But other professors of Buddhism are not so particular as the Tibetans are. And perhaps a reason for the greater strictness of the Tibetans may be found in the fellow-feeling they must have with the animals in their hard struggle against the adverse elements. When all are struggling together against the cruel cold and desolating winds a man must have some compunction at taking the life of an animal.

The Tibetan climate has been described as nearly rainless and the plateau barren and arid. Yet Tibet is also remarkable for its lakes; and these are often of great beauty. Blueness is their chief characteristic – perhaps a reflection of the brilliant azure of the Tibetan sky. Where Howard Bury's expedition left the Lhasa road to strike off westwards towards Everest is one of the most lovely of these lakes, the Bam Tso, and of peculiar beauty because it reflects in its surface the snowy range of which the famous Chomalhari is the most prominent peak.

And these lakes and meres are the haunt in summer of innumerable wild-fowl. Bar-headed geese and redshanks nest here. And families of ruddy shelducks (the Brahminy duck of India, and to be seen by all who pass by the lake in St James's Park), and gargeney teal are seen swimming in the pools. Overhead fly sand-martins, brown-headed gulls, and common terns.

Such was the country which the expedition had now to march through on its way, first to Khamba Dzong, and then Shekar and Tingri, passing occasionally through villages, for even at 15,000 feet barley and, sometimes, even wheat is grown, so warm is the sun in the short summer, but travelling for the most part through arid plains, divided from one another by ranges of hills, the outlying ridges running down from the Himalaya which was always in sight on their left.

It was while crossing one of these elevated ridges, at a height of 17,000 feet, that the first calamity to the expedition occurred. Both Kellas and Raeburn had been ill at Phari. Kellas, indeed, had been too ill to ride, and it had been necessary to carry him in a litter. But he remained cheery and no one considered that there was anything critically serious with him. It came, therefore, as a dreadful shock to the party when a man came running up excitedly to Howard Bury and Wollaston, just as they had arrived at Khamba Dzong, and announced that Kellas had died suddenly on the way: his heart had given out through weakness while being carried over the pass.

This Scottish mountaineer had, in fact, with the pertinacity of his race, pursued his heart's love till he had driven his poor body to death. He could not restrain himself. A peak was an irresistible lure. And he had worn himself out before he had even started on this expedition. He was buried on the slopes of the hill to the south of Khamba Dzong within sight of Mount Everest. And we like to know that his eyes had last rested on the scenes of his triumphs. The mighty Pauhunri, Kanchenjhow and Chomiomo, all three of which he – and he only – had climbed, rose before them on his last day's journey. So here, in the midst of the greatest mountains in the world, remains the body of this great lover of great mountains, while his ardent spirit works on, an inspiration to every other Himalayan climber.

Raeburn also was now seriously ill, and had to be sent back into Sikkim, and Wollaston had to accompany him. The climbing party was, therefore, reduced by half. Mallory and Bullock, neither of whom had been in the Himalaya before, alone remained. And Kellas's loss was the more serious because for some years he had been making a special study of the use of oxygen at high altitudes. And, at that time, many believed that it would only be by using oxygen that the summit of Mount Everest would ever be attained.

But Everest was now in sight at last, and the climbers pressed on to their goal. Across the great plain from Khamba Dzong, one hundred miles away, Everest could be seen the last of a series of peaks which included such giants as Kangchenjunga, 28,150 feet, and Makalu, 27,790 feet. There, spread out in glorious array and culminating in the highest mountain in the world, were the finest peaks in the Himalaya, only to be approached in grandeur by that other constellation of mighty peaks which cluster round K2, 28,278 feet in height, at the other end of the range.

Everest was still too distant for Mallory to make much of it from the climbing point of view. But that North-East Ridge, sloping easily downward from the summit and known to us from photographs taken near Darjiling, could be fully seen. It seemed a very feasible way up for the last fifteen hundred or two thousand feet. The question was what Everest was like below that. Was there any means of reaching that ridge? And that question could not be answered yet, for an intervening range shut out the view of the lower portion.

But, after the expedition had crossed this range and reached the basin of the Arun River, which drains the Everest glaciers and then cuts clean through the Himalaya in the most daring fashion by a series of stupendous gorges, there might be a chance of getting a satisfying view of the mountain. Starting early in the morning of June 11th Mallory and Bullock reached the banks of the river and made their way, therefore, up a rocky crest from which they fully expected to get the view they wanted.

Alas! all in the direction of Everest was cloudy vapour. Rifts, however, appeared from time to time, revealing mountain shapes behind, so they waited patiently on. And at length fleeting glimpses of a mountain which could be none other than Everest were obtained – first one fragment, then another, and then the summit itself – the great mountain face and the glacier and the ridges. And that evening from an eminence above the camp they saw the mountain again calm and clear in the closing light.

Everest was even now fifty-seven miles away and there were still intervening ridges hiding the base, but Mallory could see that the North-East Ridge was not impossibly steep, and he could see too that a valley came down from the eastern face, and evidently drained into the Arun, and might afford a means of approach. It was a valley which he was afterwards to discover and which proved to be one of the most beautiful in the whole Himalaya.

But they were not yet to prospect the mountain from this eastern side. They were to proceed further west to Tingri, rather west of north of the mountain, and bear down on it from there. Tingri was the small town visited by Rawling and Ryder in 1904. And it promised to be a convenient base of operations for the whole reconnaissance. Towards it, therefore, they continued their march.

On the way they passed Shekar Dzong which had never before been visited by a European and which is so character-istically Tibetan that it is worth while pausing, even on the verge of Everest, to hear about it. Howard Bury has given an interesting description of it, and the numerous photographs which members of all three expeditions were impelled to take bear out his description. It is finely situated on a rocky and sharp-pointed hill, like an enlarged St Michael's Mount. The actual town stands at the foot of the hill, but a large monastery, holding over four hundred monks, and consisting of innumerable buildings, is literally 'perched' halfway up the cliff. The buildings are connected by walls and towers with the fort which rises above them all. The fort again is connected by turreted walls with a curious Gothic-like structure on the summit of the hill where incense is offered up daily.

While they were resting here on June 17th Howard Bury and some of his companions visited the big monastery of Shekar Chö-te. It consisted of a great number of buildings terraced one above the other on a very steep rocky slope. A path along the face of the rock led under several archways. Then the party had to go up and down some picturesque, but very steep and narrow, streets until they came to a large courtyard on one side of which was the main temple, and in it several gilt statues of Buddha decorated all over with turquoises and other precious stones. And behind these was a huge figure of Buddha quite 50 feet high, the face of which was re-gilded every year. Around this were eight curious figures about 10 feet high, dressed in quaint flounces. They were said to be guardians of the shrine.

Ascending steep and slippery ladders, in almost pitch darkness, the party came out on a platform opposite the face of the great Buddha. Here they saw some beautifully chased silver teapots and other interesting pieces of silver richly decorated in relief. Inside the shrine it was very dark and the smell of rancid butter used in the lamps was almost overpowering.

Howard Bury and his companions were received and shown round by the official head of the monastery. And before leaving they went to see the head lama who had lived in the monastery for sixty-six years. He was looked upon as being extremely holy and as the re-incarnation of a former abbot and was practically worshipped by the people. He had only one tooth left, but for all that had a very pleasant smile. All round his room were silver-gilt chortens inlaid with turquoises and precious stones. And incense was being burnt everywhere.

This most interesting character Howard Bury was able to photograph. After much persuasion from the monks he was induced to come out dressed up in robes of beautiful golden brocades, with priceless silk Chinese hangings arranged behind him, while he sat on a raised dais with his dorje and his bell set

41

on a finely carved Chinese table in front of him. This photograph Howard Bury afterwards distributed. And no more welcome present could he give; the recipients, regarding the old abbot as a saint, would put them in shrines and burn incense in front of them.

This and other similar experiences by travellers show that religion is a very real and live and potent factor in Tibet. The chief lamas in the monasteries are often truly venerable men. The lama at Rongbuk, whom the expedition met later on, is a special instance. They have devoted their whole lives to the service of religion – and be it noted to religiously inspired art as well. On the intellectual side they are not highly developed: they have not that taste for religious philosophy that Hindus have. But they have a delicate spiritual sense. They are kindly and courteous, and are deeply venerated. And these objects of veneration satisfy a great need in the Tibetan people and perhaps account for their being so generally contented as they are. Man needs someone to worship. And here right in among the Tibetans are living beings upon which they can pour forth their adoration.

Chapter Six

THE APPROACH TO EVEREST

Tingri was reached on June 19th, and now the reconnaissance could begin in earnest. It had taken exactly a month to get there from Darjiling – longer than it takes to reach Darjiling from London – for the detour necessitated by having to avoid Nepal was a long one. But the marches across Tibet were acclimatizing the climbers for the higher altitudes to come. And from a hill behind Tingri they had a magnificent view across the plain, both of Everest itself forty-four miles away, and also of more great peaks to the west of it including those twin giants Cho Uyo, 26,867 feet, and Gyachungkang 25,990 feet.

Still, however, there were intervening ridges, for Himalayan peaks do not stick straight up by themselves. And Mallory's problem was an intricate one. He was now on the western side of that North-East Ridge which was his goal. He was looking from the opposite side to that from which it is seen from Darjiling, and he had to find out if there was any way up on to it from this north-western side, and if there were any better way to the summit than this North-East Ridge. There might be nothing but precipices and ice-falls; and, as the Duke of the

Abruzzi had found K2, Everest from its physical character might be quite unclimbable, apart from the effects of high altitude. That Mallory would have to satisfy himself about when he got closer to the mountain. His immediate task was to find some valley which would lead him to it. And this might not be easy, for all in front was a maze of mountains, and now in the monsoon season Everest itself was usually hidden.

Tingri proved to be a good base of operations. And Mallory and Bullock set out from there on June 23rd straight for Everest, while the rest of the party, including Wollaston, set out on their particular pursuits – surveying, geologizing, and collecting. The climbers took with them sixteen of the best porters and a sirdar, and having heard of a long valley leading up to Everest they made for that. Crossing a ridge, they found themselves in the valley of the Rongbuk, and ascending it they arrived on June 26th at the snout of the glacier from which it springs and in full view of Everest, only sixteen miles away, and with the high road of the glacier running straight up to it.

At these close quarters what was Everest like? This is what so many had wanted to know, and what Mallory and Bullock could now see for themselves, and at leisure. The first thing to notice about it was that it is built on big and simple lines. It has not, indeed, the smooth undulations of a snow mountain with white cap and glaciated flanks. Nor is it a broken, craggy peak, with jagged crests and pinnacles. It is rather a prodigious mountain mass – a mighty rock – coated over with a thin layer of white powder which is blown about its sides, and bearing perennial snow only on the gentler ledges and on several wide faces less steep than the rest. And the outline is comparatively smooth, because the stratification is horizontal, one great yellow band striking across the face being very conspicuous. And this circumstance seems to give strength and to emphasize the broad foundations.

From where Mallory stood two bold, well-defined ridges were presented: one was the North-East Ridge (which had been visible from near Darjiling and from Khampa Dzong), and the other was the North-West Ridge; and between these two lay the great North Face of Everest sloping steeply downward to the Rongbuk Glacier.

The spot where Mallory was encamped, and which was afterwards the site of the Base Camp, is 16,500 feet above sea level, so the climbers were already more than halfway up the mountain. It did not, therefore, have that appearance of height which it must have from the southern side, and which Kangchenjunga has from Darjiling. It was not quite 13,000 feet above the camp and appeared accordingly to be more on the Mont Blanc scale of magnitude. But there is an aspect of austerity about Mount Everest which Mont Blanc does not provide. Between it and the camp were no human habitations, no trees, no grassy meadows – hardly a living thing. All was stern rock and snow and glacier. And there were no pleasant valley breezes. Even in this valley base, and in the height of summer, the wind was fierce and biting cold.

The mountain was there before him and a way to it was at hand: the glacier itself formed a means of reaching it. And Mallory did not lose a day in proceeding up the glacier intent upon finding a way up to that North-East Ridge which he had had in his mind for so long. For the North-West Ridge, as he saw it now, was so steep near the summit as to be precluded from consideration. And he was the more drawn to this North-

East Ridge because he had noticed that from where it ends, in what may be called the North-East Shoulder, a subsidiary ridge, forming the edge of the North Face, led down probably to a col – some neck or saddle joining it to an intervening peak which shut out the view of what actually happens.

The Rongbuk Glacier proved to be more of an obstacle than a highway. But it was a surmountable obstacle and was full of strange beauty. In the higher portion it was 'a fairy world of spires'. The ice was melted into innumerable pinnacles, the largest about 50 feet in height. They resembled a topsy-turvy system of colossal icicles: icicles thrust upwards from a common icy mass, the whole resting on a definable floor.

Ascending it, the party felt a peculiar kind of lassitude which evaporated all the energy in them. It was what afterwards became known as 'glacier lassitude' and was apparently due to the amount of moisture produced by the hot sun beating on the ice and forming watery vapour in the air. Porters as well as climbers felt it.

As Mallory reached higher up and could see more of the mountain he realized that climbing Everest would be a tougher job than he had thought. The precipices which now faced him were a grim spectacle, very different from the long gentle snow slopes suggested by the photographs taken from a distance. His first idea of what the last effort would be had been that of crawling, half blind, up easy snow, on an even slope all the way from a camp to a flat snow shoulder. Now he saw it would not be that sort of grind. Climbers would be needed – and not half dazed ones. Everest was a rock mountain.

But not yet had he found a way from the glacier on to the mountain itself. So pursuing his way up the glacier he set out on July 1st to examine the head of it, right under the cliff which falls from the North-East Ridge. And here he made an important discovery. He only got a glimpse of it, owing to the amount of cloud there was about; but he saw quite distinctly the neck – what is now called the North Col – which connects the steep-sloping North Face of Everest with a peak to the north, now called the North Peak. And tumbling down from this col on to the Rongbuk Glacier was a broken glacier, or ice-fall.

This western way to the North Col *might* be a feasible way and Mallory did not write it off as absolutely impossible. But he was convinced that it should be used only as a last resort, if no other better way was to be found. The objections to it were the great height of ice-fall and the possibility of avalanches, but chiefly its exposure to the terrible west wind which prevails here. That wind would beat straight upon the climber in concentrated fury, for the glacier is in the very apex of the funnel leading up to the North Face.

More out of sheer irresistibility of mountaineering spirit than from any actual necessity, Mallory and Bullock two days later climbed a peak, afterwards named Riring, 22,520 feet high, on the western side of the Rongbuk Glacier. But from it they could see that the upper parts of the North Face lay back at no impossibly steep angle, more particularly above the North Col and up to the North-East Shoulder – the way by which all ascents were afterwards made.

The way to reach the summit was therefore now getting very much clearer. The North-East Ridge could be reached by the edge of the North Face from the North Col. From the North Col to the summit the way was clear.

The next problem was how to reach the North Col – reach it, that is to say, by a better way than that which Mallory had already seen leading up to it from the head of the Rongbuk Glacier. But before he examined that question he had one more matter to settle. There might be yet another way altogether up Everest. If he could get *behind* that long West Ridge – get round to the south of it – there might be a way there. No one had seen that side – the south-west side – and perhaps there might be a secret way up there. It was a possibility which must be gone into.

After several days' preliminary work, on July 19th he reached the summit of a col at the end of the North-West Ridge of Everest and from there looked down on to the Nepalese side of the mountain. It was a 'fantastically beautiful scene', but there was no way here. There was a big drop of about 1500 feet down to a glacier, and a hopeless precipice. He thought he might be able to traverse into the head of this glacier but found that also was impossible. And the upper part of this Western Glacier was terribly steep and broken. He could see no signs of a way up Everest from this southern side, and if there was it would have to be approached from Nepal; there was no means of getting at it from the north.

But what a sight Everest must be from this southern side, if only climbers were allowed to get there! Grand as Everest is from the north, it must be more superb still from the south. And Mallory could see a lovely group of mountains away to the south in Nepal. Was anything known of them? Their heights and position would be known, for they would have been determined, as the height and position of Everest itself was determined, by observations from the plains of India. But what beauties they must contain! What forests and flowers! And from *them* – from them looking back towards Mallory – what glories we might behold! If they had been one giant mirror and Mallory could in that mirror see backwards towards himself he would have seen what must be almost the finest view in all the world: in the foreground deep-cut forest-clad valleys, and beyond them Everest rising in tremendous precipices, with Makalu on one side and Cho Uyo on the other, and far away to east and west a continuous array of lesser, but still mighty, peaks all now glistening in the radiant sunshine, but their whiteness tinted with the purple bluey haze which prevails on the moister southern side.

And Mallory had seen other glories in this lofty region, the reconnaissance of which he had now concluded. From the summit of Riring he had seen close opposite to him on the west those two peaks Cho Uyo and Gyachungkang, both so massive and magnificent. He had also seen that less high but perhaps more beautiful peak Pumori, 23,190 feet, so attractive in its build. A vast ice-world glacier he had seen too, filled with the outpourings from these snow-clad mountains; and edging these glaciers, iron precipices, terrible in aspect.

And from all he had seen he had come to the conclusion that from this main Rongbuk Glacier which had appeared such a highway to the mountain there was no proper means of climbing Mount Everest. It was hemmed in here by such terrific precipices there was no way of approaching it – except as a last resort up that steep ice-fall to the North Col. Nor was it possible by this Rongbuk Glacier to get over to the southern side and make an attempt from there. Even if there is a way up from that side the way to it is barred by an impossible southward-facing precipice.

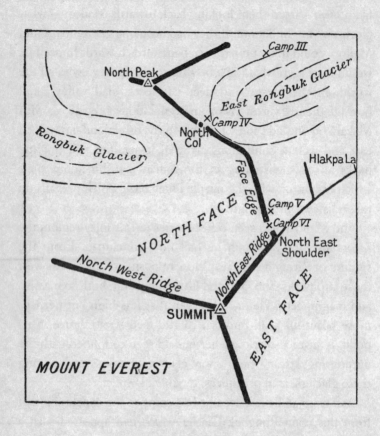

Diagram of Mount Everest

But the reconnaissance of the Rongbuk Glacier had issued in one important result: it had convinced him that the summit was accessible along the upper part of the mountain. Working downward from the summit he could see first that the North-East Ridge had a comparatively gentle slope for about three-quarters of a mile; next, that the North Face Edge leading up to this North-East Ridge from the North Col was practicable if steep. The question how to reach the North Col had not yet been solved. But once that col could be reached the way further up was practicable: on the Face Edge there was no excrescence of rock pinnacles or steep walls of rock; it was a bluntly rounded edge, comparatively smooth and continuous.

So far so good. And now Mallory and Bullock must get round to the east side of Everest, both to solve this problem of access to the North Col, and also to see if there were any better way up from there. The south side of Everest was barred. They had examined the western half of the northern approach. They must now examine the eastern portion.

Chapter Seven

THE WAY DISCOVERED

Everest had now to be approached from the east. A detour of many miles had to be made to get round the outlying spurs, in order to reach the North Col from the east, and see if it were more practicable from that side than it was from the west.

In snow and sleet and wind Mallory and Bullock struck their tents on the Rongbuk Glacier on July 25th to make for Kharta, about fifty-five miles distant by the detour, but bearing almost due east. This was the new base established by Howard Bury and was situated at the outlet of a valley running down eastward, to all appearances directly from Everest. During the month that Mallory and Bullock had been exploring the Rongbuk Glacier he had been prospecting the whole region round, and as far as the Nepal border; Morshead and Wheeler had been carrying on the survey; Heron had been geologizing; and Wollaston had been botanizing and collecting specimens of natural history. Now Kharta was to be the rallying point for the scattered members of the expedition, and here Raeburn also joined it a month later, having to some extent recovered and pluckily determined to put in what work he could for the expedition.

Kharta is situated at an elevation of only 12,300 feet; the climate was mild and there was plenty of vegetation and the people could grow crops. It was, therefore, a delicious change for Mallory and Bullock. For sublime as had been the region in which they had been working its austerity is more than man can endure for long.

We are grown accustomed to hearing of men climbing about on mountains at altitudes of 20,000 feet and more, and the climbers themselves make so little now of their breathlessness and sickness, that we are apt to forget that this is not done without strain upon them. They acclimatize themselves to these high altitudes, but the verve in them most evidently goes. A man with the fiery spirit of Mallory retains his determination. But it has become a cold hard resolve, not a joyous, ardent purpose. For the time being high altitudes do take the spring and the sheer delight in mountaineering out of a man. It becomes a drudgery which he has to drive himself to. The enjoyment of it he only gets long afterwards when the blur of fatigue and discomfort has vanished and the impressions he has received are able to shine forth in their glory.

And magnificent as the mountains are, the parts of them with which men working up a glacier come more immediately in contact, and which are all they can see when the snowy summits are hid in clouds, are often positively hideous – long bare slopes of detritus or dull rounded barren spurs. On the glacier itself they experience that curious glacier lassitude. In their little tents into which there is barely room to enter, and in which they have to sleep on the ground, they may be indifferent to discomfort for a day or two, but afterwards the cold and snow and confinement tell, and life in them becomes a weariness and worry.

Now at Kharta all this was suddenly changed. There were trees and green pastures and flowers and fields of barley. Birds and butterflies were in the air. The weather was balmy. The air was soft and warm and the sunshine bright. And the climbers did feel again some of the delight in life.

Mallory allowed himself, however, only four days of this luxury and comfort, and on August 2nd started off again for Mount Everest to tackle its eastern side. His intention had been to ascend the Kharta stream on to the glacier from which it rose. But his local guide took him out of this valley, over a pass, and down into another parallel valley on the south – into the Kama Valley. The Kharta Valley eventually proved to be the right one, as Mallory had conjectured, but it was a fortunate matter that he was led into the Kama Valley as a side excursion, for it must be the most beautiful valley in the whole Himalaya – unless forbidden Nepal has some hidden secret still more wondrous.

The beauty of the Kama Valley lay in this, that it came straight down from Mount Everest which filled in all the upper part; that it ran directly under the mighty cliffs of Makalu, a mountain not 2000 feet lower and even more beautiful than Everest; and that its fall was so rapid that while these two great peaks were in full view it had yet descended to altitudes where luxuriant vegetation was possible. From grassy meadows where cattle were grazing and gentians, primulas and saxifrages were in bloom, Everest could be seen only fifteen and Makalu only eight miles away. And those distances apply only to the summits. The outlying buttresses and precipices were much closer. A third peak also lay on the bounds of the valley – a satellite of Everest, just separated from the master mountain by a col. This was the newly discovered South Peak, now called

Hlotse, 27,890 feet. And extending from it in the direction of Makalu was a steep-faced snow-clad ridge forming a stupendous wall of glistening whiteness – but of a whiteness delicately toned by the soft blueness of the moisture-laden air.

Right opposite the climbers as they descended into the valley were the dazzling cliffs of Makalu and Chomolonzo dropping almost sheer 10,000 feet into the valley below and now powdered white with freshly fallen snow – a spectacle of perhaps unequalled mountain glory.

It was a wonderful scene for a man to come upon for the first time, and this discovery by Mallory and Bullock, Howard Bury and Wollaston a week or so later prosecuted still further, pushing on down the valley while the climbers went up it. As they made their way down this Kama Valley to its junction with the Arun Valley, just before the river cuts its way clean through the Himalaya in terrific gorges, they came, at 13,000 feet, into dense forest of juniper, silver fir, mountain ash, willow, birch and tall rhododendrons. And this only fifteen miles from the base of Mount Everest and immediately under the cliffs of Makalu. And the forest grew in beauty. The junipers with a girth of 20 feet rose to a height of 100 to 150 feet; magnolias, alders, sycamore and bamboos followed; and at scarcely twenty-three miles from the base of Mount Everest the Kama River joined the Arun at only 7500 feet above sea level.

To have discovered a valley of such varied mountain, tree, and flower-beauty would alone have been a distinction to any expedition. For many a year it will be only a few who will ever visit that secluded spot. But it will be a satisfaction to man to know that hidden there at the back of the Himalaya is a treasure for him to enjoy in times to come; and that it is one of those treasures which can never be exhausted, but which have the surprising quality that the more they are drawn upon the more there is to draw.

There is indeed another valley which may rival even this in mountain splendour. For it descends to 12,000 feet just under K2, the second highest mountain, and under its companion peaks of 27,000 and 26,000 feet in height. But this Shaksgam Valley, on the far side of the Karakoram Himalaya, more remote even than the Kama Valley, is much further north and much further removed from monsoon influence. The air is crisp and dry and cold, not soft and moist. There are no green pastures, no herds of cattle, no gentians and primulas, no combination of the lovely with the sublime. The sternness of the rugged grandeur is without alleviation.

These are the two perhaps most glorious valleys in the Himalaya – unless, as is quite likely, under Everest and Makalu on the Nepal side is something yet more splendid. But if the Shaksgam is of a harder, more unbending nature than the Kama, we need not think it is repellent. Rather do those lofty peaks challenge the intruder. They send fleeing from within him whatever is not of truest ring. But the purity and height of those sunlit summits draw him to them as a moth to the light. To see their full glory he would gladly risk his life.

Mallory and Bullock, entranced as they were with the beauty of the wonderful Kama Valley, had, however, to devote their energies to the immediate task before them of trying to find a way up to the North Col from this eastern side or any other feasible way on to the long North Ridge.

They ascended a peak on the southern side of the valley to get a full view of Everest's eastern face. It was magnificent to look upon. But upon it was a hanging glacier, and it required but little gazing, says Mallory, 'to be convinced – to know – that almost everywhere the rocks below must be exposed to ice falling from this glacier; that, if elsewhere it might be possible to climb up, the performance would be too arduous, would take too much time, and would lead to no convenient platform.'

In short, there was no way to the summit by the East Face.

It, therefore, only remained to find a way to the North Col. And Mallory could see no way on to it from this Kama Valley. But he did see that the valley he had left, the Kharta Valley, promised to disclose a way if it were followed up. He accordingly left this glorious valley for the Kharta, and ascending it to the Hlakpa La, the col at its head, did find what seemed likely to be a way to the North Col. But before he attempted to reach it he would wait till the monsoon was over and there would be a better chance of not only reaching the North Col itself but of climbing some distance up Mount Everest. This would be the climax of the whole season's work and for it proper preparation was required.

Having made this preliminary reconnaissance Mallory and Bullock returned to Kharta on August 20th for ten days' rest and reorganization. And here all the members of the expedition, including Raeburn, were by now assembled. And Wheeler had brought an important piece of information which materially affected the whole situation. In making his photographic survey of the Everest region he had discovered a glacier, now called the East Rongbuk Glacier, the stream from which joined the main Rongbuk Glacier some three miles from its terminus; and the upper portion of which probably came from the North Col. It all looks very simple now on the map. But to disentangle the lines of glaciers and ridges and sub-ridges is an extraordinarily intricate problem. Mallory had seen this stream in ascending the Rongbuk Glacier and had meant to have a look at it. But the monsoon was coming on strongly and he was pressed for time. Nor could he readily suppose that a small stream coming in from due east should derive itself from the slopes of Everest itself which was only a little east of due south. It might have come from the north or north-east instead of south. However, there it was, according to Wheeler, coming from the direction of Everest, and it might – and did – prove to be a way – and the way – by which the North Col might be reached. It was the tiny chink in the armour through which the giant could be pierced.

There were thus two possibilities which had to be investigated. The North Col might be reached from the north by the East Rongbuk Glacier, or from the east by the Kharta Glacier. These possibilities now had to be examined.

An Advanced Base Camp had already been established in the Kharta Valley on a convenient grassy plateau at about 17,300 feet; and a still higher camp at about 20,000 feet had also been pitched. And the eager Mallory had in mind not only reaching the North Col but climbing the face of Everest itself to about the North-East Shoulder. His hopes aspired even higher. Why not, he thought, establish a minute camp at 26,500 feet and then have a try for the top itself? This was his ambition. He had not yet realized how terrible is the task of climbing the supreme mountain.

On the last day of August he and Bullock were once again at

the Advanced Base up the Kharta Glacier. But there they were obliged to wait for nearly three weeks till September 19th. There was no sign of the monsoon clearing. And when at last the weather cleared it seemed unlikely that the sun would have power to melt the snow. Nothing was to be gained, however, by waiting further, and the advance was begun, though the prospects of reaching a high point on Everest were dim – so much snow was there now and so cold had it become. He determined, however, to keep to his plan until circumstances compelled him to curtail it.

His first objective was the Hlakpa La, the col at the head of the Kharta Glacier. From this he had previously looked down into what Wheeler now assured him was the upper basin of the East Rongbuk Glacier. And he meant to descend on to this glacier basin and from it climb up on to the North Col. But first he must get loads for a camp dumped on the Hlakpa La preliminary to the advance in force.

The start at an early hour on September 20th was propitious enough, and Mallory and his companion, Morshead, experienced the delight of treading snow that was both crisp and solid. They were making, too, straight for Everest and hopes were high. But it was a hard struggle through the crevasses of the glacier and over the snow of the higher part which was now of the shifting substance of fine powder. The leaders tried to stamp a firm way for the poor laden porters, but without success. The party straggled badly. But Mallory pressed on to the top of the pass to show that it could be reached. And under the inspiration of his example the little party fought its way up the final slopes and deposited eleven loads at the summit.

Mallory was now once more on the Hlakpa La, and the

weather was fine so that he could see the North Col and slopes of Everest clearly. The sight made him think. The ascent to the North Col from the glacier basin was no light matter. It was a wall of formidable dimensions, perhaps a thousand feet high, its surface was unpleasantly broken by insuperable bergschrunds; and the general angle was undoubtedly steep. It was, in fact, a hanging glacier on a huge scale. Mallory was in good hopes they would get up. But it would not be work for untrained men. And to have on the rope a number of laden porters, more or less mountain sick, conducted by only three climbers, was a proposition not to be contemplated for a moment.

A strong party would evidently be needed, and Mallory having thus prospected the way to Everest and stamped out a path up the Hlakpa La returned with the porters unladen to the high camp, where Howard Bury, Wollaston, Raeburn, Bullock and Wheeler were now assembled.

And this must have been a pleasant camp in the daytime for, though it was at an altitude of 20,000 feet, the sun was so bright and warm that the party had breakfast, lunch and tea in the open in front of their tents. Glorious views were also obtained from the top of a hill a few hundred feet above the camp, and Howard Bury describes how over the great sea of cloud which filled up the valleys all the most famous peaks could be seen rising like glistening pearly islands from a fleecy ocean. A hundred miles away to the east rose the massif of Kangchenjunga, and near by it Jannu and Chomiomo. Quite close, towering above all the rest, was Makalu, the most superb of mountains. Next to it were some of the giants of Nepal. And only a few miles to the west was Everest itself, showing sharp and clear and extra white from the fresh snow of the last month, and now no longer dwarfed by the high ridges radiating from it but standing up as a solitary peak and looking its best.

All the scene was bathed in brilliant sunshine. It was like a new world, high above the murky earth below. Everywhere was purity and light.

By September 22nd all was ready for the final advance on Everest. Raeburn had to be left behind, poor man, as he was not sufficiently recovered to stand the great hardships ahead. But the other six set out at four o'clock that morning with the thermometer showing 22 degrees of frost. Accompanying them were twenty-six coolies divided into four parties, each properly roped. It was an advance in force and there was all the thrill of nearing the crisis of the expedition.

The moon shone brightly and in the clearness of those great heights the snow-white mountains show up almost as distinctly as in the daytime, but with a peculiar ethereal appearance as if they were really fairyland. The snow on the glacier was in excellent condition. It was frozen hard and the party made excellent progress.

Then day began to dawn. Straight in front lay Mount Everest, every detail of it showing up sharp and clear in the frosty air against the deep sapphire of the western sky. And on its summit fell the first faint beams of sunlight flushing the white with pink and then slowly changing it to orange.

In the growing daylight the party made their way up the glacier by the route pioneered by Mallory, and by 10.30 they were on the summit of the Hlakpa La, 22,350 feet, with Everest only two miles away. But a steep descent of about 1200 feet on to a glacier basin below which extended to the ice wall leading up to the North Col prevented any further advance that day. And a halt had to be made on the summit. An icy wind was raging and the powdery snow which it blew off the surface penetrated everywhere. A little hollow in the snow was found a few feet from the summit and here a camp was pitched. It was the only possible place, but there was little shelter from the wind, and even the small Alpine Meade and Mummery tents were pitched with difficulty. And so much was the altitude beginning to tell that the effort of crawling into them made the occupants out of breath for some time afterwards.

It was a horrible position to be in. And the moment the sun went down the thermometer fell to 7 degrees and later on to 2 degrees below zero. The wind howled round the flimsy uncomfortable tents. No one, excepting perhaps Mallory, slept at all. In the morning all were suffering from headaches due to the want of air in the tents. And the porters were quite torpid.

With the rise of the sun and a little warm refreshment, headaches disappeared and life revived to some extent. Nevertheless, so forbidding was the aspect of the ice wall of the North Col that it was decided that only the expert Alpine climbers, Mallory, Bullock and Wheeler, should go on from here. The rest, therefore, returned to the 20,000 feet camp, while the climbers went on with a few porters.

Chapter Eight

THE NORTH COL

The North Col was the only really uncertain part in the whole way up. It was the weak link in the chain. From the summit down to the col Mallory had satisfied himself that there was no serious difficulty. From the main Rongbuk Valley Wheeler had seen that there must surely be no great difficulty in getting to the foot of the North Col. What Mallory, Wheeler and Bullock now had to ascertain was whether it was possible to get up that forbidding ice-fall that they could see from the Hlakpa La and which formed the only way on to the col – the col itself being in fact covered with this glacier in a rather peculiar fashion. They had also to decide whether this eastern climb on to the col was better or worse than the western side which Mallory had seen when ascending the Rongbuk Glacier.

This was the task before them as they left their wintry camp on the summit of the Hlakpa La on September 23rd and plunged down into the upper basin of the East Rongbuk Glacier. The descent of 1200 feet was accomplished without serious difficulty, and the party then slowly marched across the basin and pitched their tents on the open snow under the North Col at an altitude of about 22,000 feet.

Sheltered there on three sides by mountains it might have been thought that the air would have been still and that they might have passed a peaceful night. Far from it was their actual experience. Fierce squalls of wind shook and worried the tents and threatened to tear them from their moorings. And what with the annoyance of the wind and the effects of high altitude the climbers slept but little.

No very early start was possible on the 24th for the cold was great and it is hard to get men moving before sunrise at these high altitudes. And a difficult, and what might be a dangerous, task lay before the party, so only the most competent porters were taken – three in number. In half an hour the party were on the first slopes of the great ice-fall and the ascent commenced. It was a matter of climbing on snow-covered ice for a height of about 1800 feet. To an expert it was not excessively difficult; but it did require judgement. And Mallory sprang to meet the occasion as he always did when squarely faced with a mountaineering problem.

The lower part was fairly plain going. Apart from one brief spell of step-cutting when the climbers passed the corner of a bergschrund it was just straightforward plugging, first slanting up to the right on partially frozen avalanche snow, and then left, in one long upward traverse, to the summit of the col. But there was one passage shortly below the col which did cause anxiety. It was what came to be known as the final 200 feet, and just about the spot where in 1924 Mallory himself and Norton and Somervell had such difficulty in rescuing four porters marooned on the shelf just above. The snow there was lying at a very steep angle and was deep enough to be disagreeable. Some very hard work was put in by them in cutting about five hundred steps and then the worst was over. By 11.30 a.m. the party were on the North Col.

The chief obstacle in the way to the summit had now been surmounted. The way up to the North Col had not only been found but tested; and the crown had been put to the reconnaissance.

As Mallory looked from there up the North Face Edge to the North-East Ridge he could doubt no longer that it was accessible. The impressions he had gained from a distance were amply confirmed by what he saw close at hand. For a long way up those easy rock and snow slopes there was neither danger nor difficulty, as far as Mallory could see, and as indeed afterwards turned out. This then was a practicable way to the summit. It was the easiest way. And it was, indeed, in all probability the only way.

What the expedition had been sent out from England to discover had now been found. But always in their hearts the climbers had cherished the hope that perhaps they might be able to do more than find the way – they might go up it – and who knows how high? Mallory himself ardently held this hope. And he was fit enough to go higher. But the party as a whole was not fit to go much further. Wheeler thought he might be good for some more effort but had lost all feeling in his feet. Bullock was tired, but by sheer will power would have gone on – though perhaps not very much further. Mallory had slept better than the others on the two last nights, and might have done another 2000 feet, he thought. But when he had done that he would have been compelled to return in order to reach camp at the foot of the North Col before dark.

Not much more, then, could be done, and another factor

proved decisive. Even where the party stood, under the lee of a little ice cliff, the wind came in fierce gusts at frequent intervals, blowing up the powdery snow in a suffocating tourbillon. On the col beyond it was blowing a gale. And higher was a more fearful sight. The powdery fresh snow on the great face of Everest was being swept along in unbroken spindrift, and the very ridge up which the climbers' route would lie was marked out to receive its unmitigated fury. The blown snow could be seen deflected upwards for a moment where the wind met the ridge, only to rush violently down in a frightful blizzard on the leeward side. The climbers struggled on for a few moments to put the matter to the test and exposed themselves on the col to feel the full strength of the blast. But those moments were enough; they struggled back to shelter; and that was an end to climbing on Mount Everest this first season.

Wind had repelled them when that one little narrow way to the top had been found. And wind more than physical obstacles – more even than the effects of high altitudes – was to be the chief deterrent on the two subsequent expeditions. Always it had to be reckoned with. And at its worst, man could not stand against it.

Mallory had not indeed *quite* given up hope of ascending the mountain some little way. After returning to the camp at the foot of the North Col he thought over the possibility of carrying a small camp on to the North Col. But rations were short and porters not willing and if there were any mishap there would be in rear that heavy climb up 1200 feet to the Hlakpa La. And what chance was there of the wind abating? None whatever.

Nothing further then was possible. And nothing further was necessary; for they had already accomplished what they had been sent out to do. They had found a practicable route to the summit, and they had tested that part of it which would be the most difficult from a climbing point of view, apart from the effects of high altitude. And all this they had done in spite of the loss of the two most experienced climbers and the only two who had previously known the Himalaya. So they returned to the main camp.

With the return journey to India we need not trouble. Under Howard Bury's leadership the objects of the expedition had been fully attained. Besides finding the way up the mountain the whole Everest region had been mapped, and a particular survey had been made of the immediate neighbourhood of the mountain. A geological survey had also been made, and the natural history studied and specimens collected. And within a year of the expedition starting from Darjiling a book was published containing the reports and maps ready for the use of the second expedition.

The foundation was well and truly laid; and the two succeeding expeditions fully acknowledged their indebtedness to the good work put in by this first reconnaissance.

Chapter Nine

PREPARING AGAIN

A real attempt to reach the summit might now be made – a real all-out effort. The mountain had been prospected; the path had been pioneered; a way up – perhaps the only feasible way – had been found; and effort could now be concentrated on the supreme aim of reaching the top.

A fresh expedition constituted for this one purpose must be organized. A new permission from the Tibetan government was applied for and, when this was received and Howard Bury and his party had returned, preparations were made at speed. And there was no time to lose, for it was evident from Mallory's reports that the climb should be made *before* the monsoon broke. It breaks early in June. In the last fortnight of May and the first week of June the climbers should be on the mountain. This would mean that the expedition must leave Darjiling before the end of March. For this to be possible stores and equipment must be got away from England in January 1922. And it was now November, 1921. Speed therefore was needed.

But the all-important question of leadership had first to be decided. Howard Bury had done so much and had done it so well that it was hard to ask him to stand down. In the diplomatic preliminaries on his first mission to India and now in the general conduct of the expedition, the overcoming of grave transport difficulties which had arisen, the arrangement for supplies, the delicate dealings with the Tibetans, and the strategy of the entire reconnaissance, he had shown so much proficiency and tact, and he must have looked forward so keenly to reaping the final fruit of all his endeavours, that it must have been a cruel strain on himself now to give way. But the conquest of Everest demands, time after time, the sacrifice of the individual for the common purpose. There was now available a man pre-eminently fitted for the leadership, and Howard Bury chivalrously accepted what was clearly so desirable in the interest of the whole enterprise.

Brigadier General Hon C. G. Bruce, on his retirement from service in India, had received an appointment in the Territorial Force and could not join the first expedition, but now he was able to obtain leave. He was too old to be one of the climbers. And it is doubtful whether at any time he would have been able to reach the summit, for experience has shown that it is men of a lighter, slimmer build, with less weight to carry, who go highest on Everest. But no better leader for the whole expedition could be found; for his experience of the Himalaya and Himalayan people is unequalled. He had belonged to a Gurkha regiment and been stationed in the Himalaya nearly all his service – and Gurkhas are inhabitants of Nepal in which half of Everest lies. He had been a member of many Himalayan expeditions, from Sir Martin Conway's of 1892 onward. He had also exerted himself to learn the craft of mountaineering in the Alps; and he had taken Gurkhas there too. And he had such a knowledge of these hill peoples, such an understanding of them, such a way with them, that he could get more out of them than any other living man. He was devoted to them and they adored him. And as the English climbers would be absolutely dependent on these men to carry a light camp high enough to make the final dash for the top possible, Bruce's influence with them was of priceless value to the expedition. And the same characteristics which enabled him to exert this influence with the simple hill men made him also an ideal leader of any expedition.

For he is an extraordinary mixture of boy and man. You never know whether it is a boy or a man whom you are talking to. If he lives to be a hundred he will always be a boy; and as a boy he must always have been a man. He is a boisterous boy, perpetually effervescing with boyish fun. And he is a shrewd, competent man who will not stand the slightest nonsense. A remarkable and very effective combination. He has that pluck, too, which will never allow his spirits to be depressed. And these spirits are infectious; the whole party catches them. That is why he is so acceptable as a leader. Any party with Bruce in it would be a cheery party – and being cheery would be able to do its work to best advantage.

Many are the stories of Bruce. One is that, when a dispute arose on a certain expedition as to who was above who, Bruce said, 'Well, I'm only a coolie,' and took up a load and carried it. Which is very similar to a story about another great mountaineer, the Duke of the Abruzzi, on his expedition in Alaska, who, when the men were objecting to carrying loads, shamed them into doing it by strapping one on his own back and carrying it a whole stage.

This is the man who was now invited to lead the expedition;

and, with his aid, the actual climbers had then to be selected. Fortunately Mallory would be again available, but Bullock had to return to his consular duties and watch proceedings from the comfortable haven of Havre. Finch had now recovered and in him the expedition would have an expert mountaineer of great experience, for he had spent much of his youth in Switzerland and climbed in winter as well as summer. And even Mallory could not surpass him in keenness and determination to conquer Everest. These two had been considered before. Two new climbers in England to be invited to join were Norton and Somervell.

Major (now Lieutenant Colonel) E. F. Norton, DSO, was well known in the Alpine Club and was well versed in the lore of mountaineering. He had the additional advantage of having served in India and been on shooting expeditions in the Himalaya. He could speak Hindustani and knew how to handle Indian peoples. Compact and collected, erect and direct, and with a habit of command, he inspired confidence at once. And there was a kindliness and suavity about him which increased the trust placed in him. He was indeed a combination of many qualities. As an officer of the Royal Horse Artillery he was noted for the smartness of his battery; he had served with distinction in the war; he had passed the Staff College; for seven years he had run the Kadir Cup Meeting – the great pig-sticking event in India; he was a keen observer of birds; and he was an amateur painter of more than average ability. In everything he was methodical and in hand. And in his punctuality he took great pride: he would be neither too early nor too late. It was not much more than a minute before the train left Victoria that he arrived at the station on his way to India and he was leisurely saying goodbye to his friends and the train was well on the move as he quietly stepped into it continuing his conversation. With him there would be no flurry in emergency. Forethought would have provided for every contingency. And when the ultimate moment came one might be certain he would put all his well-saved energies into the decisive action.

No less – perhaps even more – versatile was Howard Somervell. A surgeon by profession, he was a skilled and daring mountaineer, and also a painter and a musician, of no mean talent. An inhabitant of the Lake District, he had been with hills all his life and loved them. He was a man of great resolution and great fortitude and great energy and stamina. But over and above this he was a man of a great and a stout and a warm heart – the kind of ready, open, accessible man that every other man feels at once at home with; and a dependable handy man who would be all there when a hard turn had to be done. A big strong man – not in body but in disposition, and with abounding buoyancy. In body there was nothing particular to meet the eye. He certainly had not the erectness of Norton nor the huge strength of Bruce. And he was not wiry. Perhaps suppleness was its chief characteristic – as it was a characteristic of his mind – the suppleness of a spring, with readiness to yield but tenacity to return.

Somervell is a writer as well as everything else, and publishers should be on the lookout for the book he will write on Everest twenty years hence when the mightiest impressions have had time to make themselves felt to the full. A man of science, a man of art, a man of warm humanity, and a man of strong religious feeling, he should have something worth saying when memories of physical suffering have faded away and the spirituality of the whole adventure has had time to mature in his mind.

Mallory and Finch, Norton and Somervell – these were the climbers who could be counted on to go highest. Then came Colonel E. L. Strutt, DSO, Dr Wakefield, Captain Geoffrey Bruce, and Mr C. G. Crawford of the Indian Civil Service who, because they were either too old for the highest strain or had not yet sufficient mountaineering experience, would form the support.

Strutt was a man of great experience in the Alps and of the type for the top if he could have been on Everest a few years earlier. He would be invaluable as second-in-command and in charge of the expedition when it left the Base Camp where Bruce would remain.

Wakefield, like Somervell, came from the Lake District and as a young man had there performed prodigious feats of mountaineering. He was now in practice in Canada, but so desperately keen on joining the expedition that he sold his practice and came over.

Geoffrey Bruce was a younger cousin of General Bruce and was not technically trained in mountaineering. But he had been about in the Himalaya and belonged to a Gurkha Regiment; so he would be helpful with the Nepalese and Tibetans, and available at a pinch to climb with the more experienced mountaineers.

Crawford was a daring rock climber and serving in the hill districts of India had become enthusiastic about the idea of climbing Everest. And his knowledge of the language and ways of the people would also be a help.

Then as doctor and naturalist came that veteran Himalayan climber, Dr T. G. Longstaff, who still holds the record for having attained a higher *summit* than anyone else. Others have climbed higher than he has on the sides of mountains. But no one has reached a higher summit than Trisul, 23,406 feet, which he climbed in 1907. He had also discovered a wonderful glacier region in the Karakoram Himalaya. And his wide experience in the Alps and the Himalaya made his judgement on situations and conditions a valuable contribution to the expedition. His genial enthusiastic nature was an additional contribution of value.

And this time the expedition was to have an official photographer. Captain J. B. Noel had made a journey from Sikkim in the direction of Mount Everest in 1913, and ever since had interested himself in the idea of climbing the mountain. He had also interested himself in photography and become an expert in the art, and especially in cinematography. He gave up the army and joined the expedition. Perhaps *his* chief characteristic was always being up to the occasion. When most wanted Noel would be there – when most wanted as a man, that is, not necessarily as a photographer. He also had great pertinacity and was a devoted lover of mountain beauty.

There was an idea of getting an artist of distinction to accompany the expedition to paint the wonderful mountain scenery. It is true that Everest from the Base Camp is no more imposing than Mont Blanc from many standpoints. The Base Camp is itself so high that Everest does not rise higher above it than Mont Blanc or Mont Rosa rise above the lower valleys. Still it has the fascination which attaches to the highest mountain in the world. Also, from the Kama Valley, Everest and Makalu must present an appearance unequalled by any mountain in Europe. And if the Tibetan plains and the lower slopes of the Tibetan mountains are arid, bare and uninteresting, yet with the monsoon comes the haze which transfigures plain and mountain and afterwards made Somervell despair of finding in his pallet a blue of sufficient brilliance and intensity to reproduce the colour of the shadows twenty or thirty miles away. There was evidently in the Everest region scope for a painter of the very first rank. And on the way up to Tibet through Sikkim there was mountain and forest scenery on the grandest possible scale. However, no artist of the front rank, possessed of the physique for the journey, could be found. So the expedition had to depend on Noel's photographs and Somervell's pictures, painted in hurried moments snatched from climbing, to reproduce the impressions the mountains made.

While all these preparations were in progress a thorny question was raised. Why not use oxygen? Kellas had started experiments in the use of oxygen for climbing. Why not continue them? The one serious obstacle to attaining the summit of the mountain was the lack of oxygen in the air. Supply that want and the climbers would be up it tomorrow.

So far the Everest Committee had not thought of equipping the expedition with oxygen, because there had been doubt as to the possibility of supplying it in any portable form. And then there was just a suspicion at the back of men's minds that it was not exactly sporting to use it. It could be argued of course that inhaling oxygen was no more unsporting than taking a nip of brandy or a cup of beef-tea. But there the fact remained that a man who got up without oxygen would be looked upon as having done a finer deed than the man who climbed Everest using oxygen. We would not ask a man if he had stimulated himself with tea on the way up as long as he had reached the summit. But if he had used oxygen we would certainly rate his achievement lower than if he had used only the usual stimulants. There was, therefore, a prejudice against using oxygen. And the committee shared it. They did subsequently abandon this prejudice, but they might have done better to retain it. For by not using oxygen it has been proved that men's bodies do adjust themselves to the unusual conditions. Men get 'acclimatized' and can ascend to 28,000 feet, as they have shown.

However, this much was not known in 1922 when the preparations were being made. Then no man had ascended higher than 24,600 feet. To many scientific men it seemed impossible that the summit would ever be attained without some adventitious aid. And many mountaineers, and among the new members of the expedition, notably Finch, were in favour of its use. If you want to make certain of reaching the summit, use oxygen, they said. And when Somervell made a very powerful and persuasive appeal for its use the committee finally and unanimously agreed.

Yet it was a hesitating agreement. And it may be doubted whether it was a wise one. Beyond one or two members the expedition as a whole was never thoroughly keen on its use. The apparatus was heavy and unwieldy; and Somervell himself did not use it. And unless there were real faith in it oxygen was not likely to be successful.

The consideration that weighed most with the committee was that an oxygen pair might be able to pioneer the way for a non-oxygen pair. It might be easier to get to 26,000, 27,000 feet or whatever was the altitude aimed at *with* oxygen; and then the way having once been trodden others would follow more readily. In actual practice it turned out the other way round in every instance. Always it was the non-oxygen men who led the way.

There is such a thing as being too much dependent on science and too little dependent on the human spirit. Everest stands for an adventure of the spirit. And things might have gone better if faith in the spirit had been stronger.

Chapter Ten

THE SECOND START

By March 1st, 1922, Bruce was at Darjiling. He had left England ahead of the rest in order to make preparations. Now he was in his element: he was in the Indian 'hills' again, and he was surrounded by hill folk. Mr Wetherall, the agent, had been making a number of preliminary arrangements, repairing the tents of the last expedition, buying up flour, rice and other local stores; and a hundred and fifty hill men – Sherpas, Bhotias and others from this borderland of Nepal and Tibet – had been collected from whom Bruce would select the porter corps, in accordance with his own sound idea. And there was plenty of competition for inclusion in the expedition, for these hill men have great hardihood and plenty of the spirit of adventure when they are with a Sahib whom they can trust. So Bruce got together a good useful lot. Then he instilled into them a sense of the honour which would be theirs and the name they would make if the expedition were successful. And this appeal to their spirit, as well as the good pay, good clothes and good food promised, enlisted them enthusiastically in the enterprise. They enjoyed the feeling of fellowship in a big adventure.

But high-spirited as they are, they have also their foibles, as

Bruce well knew. They are light-hearted and irresponsible as children, and when drink is accessible they take very kindly to it. So in reinforcement of his own stern warnings he got their priests to warn them too. And before they left both Brahmins and Buddhist priests gave them their blessing – a thing on which they set much store. Possibly their religion is not very refined; but, like all men who live in close and constant touch with nature, they have a sense of dependence on some mighty and mysterious power behind things; they have great reverence for priests and holy men who in some vague way represent that power to them; and they feel reinforced and happy if they have the goodwill of this representative.

Another matter to which Bruce paid special attention was the choice of cooks. He was like a father to the expedition in this and many other ways, and having seen how much the last expedition had suffered through bad and filthy cooking he had up a number of cooks, took them out into the hills, and tested them before selecting four of the best.

And in all this work he was now assisted by Geoffrey Bruce and by Captain Morris, another officer from a Gurkha Regiment who could speak Nepalese and knew how to handle these hill men.

Four Gurkha non-commissioned officers and a Gurkha orderly had also been lent for the service of the expedition by the Commander-in-Chief, Lord Rawlinson.

An interpreter also was enlisted – a young Tibetan educated in Darjiling, named Karma Paul. He turned out a complete success and Bruce speaks of him as having been 'always good company, and always cheerful'. He had excellent manners and a good way with the Tibetans. And this must have counted for much; for the Tibetans, like all Eastern peoples, have excellent manners themselves, and are very amenable to good manners in others. A coarse-mannered interpreter might have wrecked the expedition.

Besides the climbers from England who reached Darjiling during March, Mr C. G. Crawford from Assam now joined. And Major Morshead, full of enthusiasm, was able to obtain leave and come not as a survey officer but as a member of the expedition.

Thus the second expedition was finally completed, though the oxygen apparatus did not arrive for some days later. The whole of the party were entertained by the Buddhist Association and the Hillmen's Association, under the presidency of Mr Laden La, the Deputy-Superintendent of Police; and the chief Lamas and Brahmins of the district blessed the party and offered up prayers for its well-being and success. And on March 26th the expedition started from Darjiling with the good wishes of every one there.

The trek through Sikkim and across Tibet to the Base Camp in the Rongbuk Valley need be very briefly described. The second expedition followed nearly the same route as the first. But being two months earlier they experienced severer weather. The rhododendrons which form one of the chief glories of Sikkim were not in flower. And when they arrived at Phari on April 6th the winter was scarcely over. Leaving again on the 8th they crossed the Tang La in heavy snow with the wind blowing nearly a hurricane. They made for Khampa Dzong by a shorter route, but had to cross a pass 17,000 feet high with a howling wind blowing straight down from the ice fields of the Himalaya.

On arrival there on April 11th they found Kellas's grave in good order with a clean-cut inscription in English and Tibetan on it, and they made their reverence to his memory by adding a few more great stones. Then they marched for Shekar, which they reached on April 24th, and again visited the great lama of the place. But Bruce was not so impressed by him as his predecessors had been. He thought him an extremely cunning old person and a first-class trader. He had immense collections of Tibetan and Chinese curios and knew the price of them as well as any professional dealer. And the rest of the lamas were the dirtiest crowd Bruce had met in Tibet – which must be saying a good deal, for he had passed through Phari.

With the lama at Rongbuk Monastery, which he reached on April 30th, Bruce was, however, very differently impressed. The monastery is situated in full view of Everest, only sixteen miles distant. And the lama is regarded as the incarnation of the god Chongraysay. He was about sixty years of age, 'full of dignity, with a most intelligent and wise face and an extra-ordinarily attractive smile'. The people treated him with the utmost respect, and he on his part was particular in asking Bruce that he should be kind to the people. He was also particular about the animals. No life may be taken in this region and the wild animals are fed; so that the wild sheep, so hard to approach on the Indian side of the Himalaya, were here almost tame, and came quite close to the camp.

But why Englishmen should want to climb Everest was a puzzle to the lama. He questioned Bruce closely as to the objects of the expedition; and Bruce gave him a very sensible reply. He said that they were on a pilgrimage. It was the only way of conveying to such people the simple fact that the expedition was out for no material object, like finding gold or coal or diamonds, but for a spiritual object – the quickening of the human spirit. There was in England, he explained, a sect which worshipped mountains and they were come out to worship the highest mountain in the world. And, if by worship is meant intense admiration, nothing could be truer than Bruce's way of putting it.

Higher up the valley were six or seven hermits' dwellings. The cells were very small and the devout occupants never have any firing or warm drinks. They are fed from the monasteries and spend the years in contemplation of the Ōm – the Godhead. Here at over 16,000 feet above sea level in a Tibetan winter they must suffer terribly; but Tibetans have incredible powers of endurance; and, contrary to one's expectations, these hermits do not all have their natures numbed – some at least come out of their ordeal with very kindly and sensitive natures.

These were the last human habitations, and on May 1st, punctual to programme, Bruce brought the expedition, consisting of thirteen British, between forty and fifty Nepalese and others, and about a hundred Tibetans and three hundred yaks, to the snout of the Rongbuk Glacier where the Base Camp was to be formed in full view of Everest.

The mountain might well have been surprised at so vast an invasion. And the battle with it was now to begin in earnest. With the exception of Finch the expedition had arrived in good health this time. Attention to the cooking had had its good results. And the month's march across Tibet, though wearisome from the incessant biting winds and the constant sight of arid plains and monotonous hills, had also done good in hardening and acclimatizing the climbers. Too much physical exertion at these high altitudes is apt to detract from, rather than increase, their fitness and Bruce, therefore, encouraged them to ride rather than walk most of the way. But they had walked quite enough to keep themselves fit and were now eager to tackle the mountain in that short interval, of about three weeks only, between the excessive cold of winter and the advent of the monsoon, when alone it is assailable. Just by one narrow strip in space and for one short moment in time is the mountain vulnerable. But at that point in space and that moment in time she *is* vulnerable. And there and then the assailants meant to press home to the utmost of their strength.

What they had to aim at was getting two tiny tents carried up the North Face to some niche near the North-East Ridge at a height of 27,000 feet. If *that* could be done, then four climbers could sleep the night there, and issuing forth on the following morning have a good chance of covering the remaining 2000 feet to the summit. *More* than 2000 feet from the summit they were unlikely to be able to do in one day. The rate at which climbers can ascend diminishes rapidly as altitude increases. So the crux of the situation was the capacity of porters to carry two tents with sleeping bags, provisions and light cooking apparatus, for this 27,000 feet camp.

It was a big thing to ask of them. For up to this time even *un*laden men had not ascended higher than 24,600 feet. And that extra 2400 feet to be climbed by *laden* men might well prove the last straw. But unless the porters could do it there was little chance of the climbers reaching the top. It is true, one tent instead of two might possibly be carried, and two climbers instead of four might make the final effort. But this would be risky. One might be taken ill or have an accident and the other be incapable of bringing him back. Four climbers for the last 2000 feet, and therefore two tents at 27,000 feet was the object to aim at.

And if this were to be done there must be a camp at 25,000 feet, intermediate between the highest camp and the North Col Camp at 23,000 feet; and between the North Col Camp and the Base Camp a string of probably three camps on the east Rongbuk Glacier which was the way by which the North Col was to be approached. And the carrying of tents for these camps, carrying the flour, meat and other provisions for the climbers and porters, carrying the yak dung fuel, and carrying all the other paraphernalia of camp life necessitated the employment of much transport in some form or other. On the high camps above the glacier only Bruce's special porter corps could be used. But this work alone would try them to the utmost. Bruce was, therefore, particularly anxious to get local men or animals for work on the glacier, so that the forty Nepalese porters would be free for the great effort on the mountain itself.

This was the theoretically ideal arrangement to be aimed at. On such occasions nothing ever does go exactly as you plan it. But you have at least to shape it in your mind and then get as near to it as you can. And Bruce for the last few marches before reaching the Base Camp had been working it out. He had been trying to induce a hundred Tibetans to come on beyond the Base Camp and work on the glacier. He thought he had persuaded ninety. But when it came to the point these dwindled to forty-five; and even these worked for only two days and then went home. The fact is May is the ploughing time in Tibet and they were badly wanted on their fields. The good pay offered them was no sufficient inducement. And there was not much to be made out of an appeal to their love of fame and honour for, after all, there is *not* much fame to be got out of carrying tents and stores up a glacier.

But this failure to secure local men was nearly, and might have proved quite, a fatal blow to the expedition. If Bruce had not had the wisdom to bring a corps of porters of his own there would have been no ascent of Everest at all. As it was, the original plan had to be considerably curtailed. And he might have had to curtail it still more if he had not been able to arrange for a succession of carriers to come in from the nearest village for a day or two's work at a time. In this way both men and women came – the women often carrying babies. Thus a stream of local carriers was maintained for the service of Camp I and II on the glacier, though they would not go higher. And again one has to marvel at the hardihood of these Tibetans, for even the women and children would sleep out under rocks at 16,000 feet and 17,000 feet.

Meanwhile Strutt, Longstaff, and Morshead had been dispatched to reconnoitre the East Rongbuk Glacier. For it will be remembered that Mallory had only seen it at the head and Wheeler only at the end, and no one had actually ascended it through its whole course. A way up it had to be found – and the best way up it – and sites for camps located at the most suitable spots.

It was a strange and weird world that Strutt and his companions entered. The East Rongbuk Glacier in its middle region is broken, or rather melted, into a sea of icy pinnacles of amazingly fantastic shapes – glistening white on the surface in the sun and often also of a translucent blue or green where caves have been eroded in them.

An excellent site for Camp I was found, and here Geoffrey Bruce erected a number of stone huts and used the spare parts of tents as roofs. The walls gave some shelter at least from the wind, though they might have been considered draughty by the fastidious. This camp was at an altitude of 17,800 feet, and was at a distance of about three hours' journey from the Base Camp.

Two thousand feet higher up the glacier was Camp II, about four hours' journey from Camp I. This second camp was situated under a wall of ice close to the most fantastic part of this astonishing world of ice. Beyond this, as the higher part is reached, the pinnacles gradually merged in the tumbled ice river of the glacier. But the gradient was not steep and the ice was not an ice-fall.

Camp III was fixed at a site on the moraine at about 21,000 feet, and four hours from Camp II. It lay under the shelter of the North Peak and had the advantage of the morning sun, as it faced east. But the sun was off it soon after three, and the evenings were chill and dreary.

Strutt's party arriving there so early in May experienced intense cold and suffered from the usual biting wind; and Longstaff, who had not been at his best for some time, was incapacitated from any further high altitude work that season. On May 9th the three returned to the Base Camp after establishing cooks at each camp for the benefit of parties who would now be continually passing up and down.

The glacier reconnaissance being completed, glacier camps established and supplies pushed up to Camp III to enable climbers actually to ascend the North Col and pitch a camp on it, the climbers now moved forward for the attack. It was still a trifle early in the season. But the exact date when the monsoon will break can never be predicted, and the earliest chance for a climb must be seized. On May 10th, therefore, Mallory and Somervell left the Base Camp and in two and a half hours arrived at Camp I, where they found themselves in a 'house' and were welcomed by a cook offering them some tea. And so in comparative comfort they arrived at Camp III, where their real work would begin. Theoretically, these two superb mountaineers, the very pick of the whole party, should have been kept in reserve longer yet. Less good men than they were should have been employed in preparing the way, while these two were kept in clover at the base, or in one of the glacier camps, exercising and acclimatizing themselves by ascents of the mountains round, but always having a comfortable camp to return to for good food and refreshment and shelter, while all the drudgery on ahead was being done for them by others. Then, when the way was all smooth, they would have passed easily, rapidly and comfortably through and be in the best possible condition for making the supreme effort upon which all else depended. This is what theoretically should have been done. But, again, theory had to be abandoned.

As Mallory had discovered in the previous year, the ascent to the North Col was the stiffest and most dangerous part of the whole way up to the summit. It was a wall and slope of ice and snow, seamed with crevasses and liable to avalanches. Only experienced mountaineers could tackle such an obstacle. And in the whole party only four, or perhaps five, were at the moment fit to be trusted with the task. These four were Mallory and Somervell, Finch and Norton. And the latter two being reserved for the oxygen attack, it fell out that Mallory

and Somervell had now to tackle this surmountable but difficult and dangerous obstacle.

This was Somervell's first entry into the higher regions of
the Himalaya; and bursting with energy he set off the same
afternoon that they arrived at Camp III to climb a col just
opposite the camp on his usual quest for beauty. And there
indeed he found it. For, from this Rápiu La, as the col is called,
he looked down into the wonderful Kama Valley and on to
that superb peak, Makalu. He hurriedly made a sketch – or
jotted down indications for a sketch – and was back with
Mallory at 5.30.

The next day, May 13th, Mallory and Somervell, with one
porter carrying one tent, some spare rope and wooden pegs, set
out from Camp III to pioneer the way up to the North Col and
make the establishment of a camp there possible. A way had to
be found which would be safe – or could be made safe – for a
continual stream of porters going up and down carrying
supplies for the higher camps. And the finding of such a way
and making it secure required some thinking out. Mallory, of
course, had been up this wall before. But, since he was there in
the previous autumn, changes had occurred. The way he had
ascended in soft snow was now glittering with a glitter that told
of blue ice, bare and hard. This would never do. A different way
had to be found. To the left was a hopeless series of impassable
ice cliffs. To the right were some very steep ice slopes for three
or four hundred feet and beyond a sloping corridor apparently
well covered with snow. Step-cutting was necessary up the ice
slopes, and for future use by porters ropes were fixed. But
beyond, up to the col itself, though the slope steepened, there
was nothing to impede.

The North Col was reached without mishap. A way secure for porters had been made. A minute tent had been pitched as a token of conquest. And now they had time to enjoy the view. They were at 23,000 feet altitude, 7000 feet higher than Mont Blanc, and an extensive view was due to them. But Everest was towering still 6000 feet above them on one side and the North Peak 2000 feet above them on the other. So their vision was still confined. But they did have a perfect view of the beautiful north-west side of Everest with its glistening wall of ice and rugged precipices; and of that very perfect peak Pumori.

Pumori is only a pigmy among the giants of this region. It is but 23,000 feet in height. But it is very beautiful in form. Its snowcap, says Mallory, 'is supported by splendid architecture; the pyramidal bulk of the mountain, the steep fall of the ridges and faces to the south and west, the precipices of rock and ice towards east and north are set off by a whole chain of mountains, extending west-north-west along a frail, fantastic ridge unrivalled anywhere in the district for the elegant beauty of its cornices and towers'.

Such a view is some compensation for hard toil. But on the whole Everest climbers had little reward in the shape of enjoyment of beauty for their labours. For their way led them up a confined valley and the lower portions of these mountains are often frankly ugly. They are far above the line of life. No tree or shrub or patch of green is seen. Where there is not ice and snow and precipice there are often long slopes of hideous debris.

Leaving the tent as a sign of occupation Mallory and Somervell with the unladen porter descended the same after-noon to Camp III. They had felt the altitude to some extent, but after a couple of days' rest they recovered quickly, and were so full of zeal to accomplish the great task before them that they even contemplated doing without a tent above the North Col – an idea which was fortunately never put into practice, for it is doubtful whether any man could spend the night on the face of Everest and survive. In any case, it would be only on a perfectly windless night that it would be at all likely. And perfectly windless nights are usually extremely cold nights. So that if a man escaped death from the wind he might perish from the cold. Later experience showed that even inside a tent the wind and cold were almost unbearable.

On May 16th Camp III was reinforced by the arrival of Strutt, Morshead, Norton, and Crawford, and a large convoy of stores. May was now half over. The three weeks in which alone in all the year the mountain is vulnerable had arrived. And the party were further incited to immediate action by what Mallory reported he had seen on the 16th from the Rápiu La. Looking down into the Kama Valley he had seen that 'the clouds boiling up in that vast and terrible cauldron were not gleaming white but sadly grey'. Trouble was in store, he concluded. The monsoon was at hand. They must race against it; and make for the summit while yet they could.

Accordingly, on the next morning, May 17th, without waiting a day longer, Strutt, Mallory, Somervell, Norton, and Morshead with the porters (each carrying from 25 to 30 lb) set out for the North Col, while Crawford, who was ill, had to return to the base. On the slope up there was no wind and the party even felt the heat and glare of the morning sun beating direct on them. But Mallory and Somervell felt the altitude less than on their first ascent. They were becoming acclimatized.

And perhaps this fact, that men do adjust themselves to the new conditions of high altitude, is a good reason for not keeping the climbers designated for the final effort too low down. It may be well for them to have some days at 21,000 and 23,000 feet before they strike off higher.

May 18th was spent in rest at Camp IV on the North Col and in forming the camp. The following day the second lot of loads arrived and the climbers were now established in reasonably comfortable conditions. Their tents were indeed pitched on snow, for there was no rock or debris available; but they were sheltered by huge masses of ice from the bitter west wind; and they had food in plenty and in great variety – tea, cocoa, peasoup, biscuits, ham, cheese, sausages, sardines, herrings, bacon, ox-tongues, jam, chocolate, Army and Navy rations, and spaghetti. As far as solid food was concerned, nothing had been overlooked. The difficulty was water. On the North Col and upward the snow and ice never melt: they simply evaporate. There is therefore no stream or trickle anywhere. For water snow had to be laboriously melted on this and the other high camps.

On May 20th the ascent of the actual mountain was to begin.

Chapter Eleven

THE ATTACK

On the vigil of the great adventure Mallory was full of hope. If with their slender arrangements he did not actually expect to reach the summit, at any rate he hoped to. But all must necessarily depend upon how high the porters would be able to carry a camp. Not 'all', perhaps, for even if the porters carried a tent or tents to 27,000 feet, the climbers might not be able to accomplish the last 2000 feet. Still, if the porters could not carry a camp to somewhere near 27,000 feet, there would be little hope for the climbers.

Nine porters only were available on the morning of May 20th, and of these only four were really fit. Two tents weighing 15 lb each were to be carried, together with two double sleeping bags, feeding utensils, and provisions for one and a half days. This made only four loads of 20 lb each for the nine porters. It was giving the porters every possible chance, and of course they were men from these mountains, and accustomed all their lives to carrying loads.

The climbers were Mallory, Somervell, Norton and Morshead. Strutt was to return to Camp III; he had not acclimatized well.

The start was made at 7.30, and now for the first time in its history man stood actually on the mountain itself. Long millions of years ago there must have been teeming life upon it; for it was once below the sea, and later must have been a tropical island, covered with palms and ferns, and swarming with bird and insect life. But this would have been before the appearance of man; and during all the history of man it must have been a snow-clad mountain. And if the Nepalese and Tibetans have never had the enterprise to climb it we may be sure that primitive man never would have. May 20th, 1922, may therefore be taken as the date on which man first set foot on Everest. But history has not yet recorded with certainty which of the four climbers was actually the first to plant his foot on the slope leading up the mountain from the North Col. Morshead is, however, mentioned as leading at first; so, perhaps, the honour is his. And this would be most fitting, as he belongs to that service, the Survey of India, which first discovered and determined the height and position of the mountain and which then named it after their former Chief, the Surveyor-General, Sir George Everest.

And what was the mountain like now that the climbers were at close grip with it? From a distance it had looked accessible: was it accessible under the proof? Looking up the North Face from its foot the slope is slightly concave, steepening as the North-East Ridge is approached. The climbers may either follow the rounded edge of the face as it joins with the north-east face to the left or find a parallel way on the gently receding face on the right. In either case the going was not difficult. And in one part there was a big patch of snow which afforded a convenient way. The difficulty lay not in the mountain itself but in the cold and the effects of altitude. The morning had been calm and fine, which was fortunate, as on other occasions climbers have found a terrible wind here. But 1200 feet up the air had become very cold and they put on more clothes. The sun now disappeared behind clouds. The cold increased as they climbed higher. Altitude was beginning to tell and they had to struggle hard for breath, taking several breaths between each step.

By 11.30 they were at 25,000 feet; and here a difficulty arose. They had intended to proceed to 26,000 feet. But the question was: where would they find space for even the tiny tents they had? The rocks were all dipping steeply; and where the ground was broken the ledges were too steep to hold a tent. They were in a serious predicament. They must find a spot somewhere for their tents, and must find it in time to allow the porters to return to the North Col before the weather grew worse, for the two tents carried were only sufficient for the climbers. They scoured the mountain, especially on the lee side, over the edge of the face, for some place sufficiently flat and sufficiently commodious to hold a tent. Clouds prevented any extensive view and they had to poke about near at hand. At last, about two o'clock, Somervell and some porters found a place for one tent. For the second the least unlikely place was chosen and the most made of it: it was at the foot of a long sloping slab. On it a platform was built up and the tent pitched. And at three the porters were sent down to the North Col.

The difficulty the climbers had – and the next expedition had the same experience – in finding even the small space of level ground required for one of these little tents is a good illustration of the kind of surface the mountain presented. The face of Everest was not precipitous; but it was steep – and continuously steep.

The night was fairly warm and the thermometer did not fall below 7 degrees, and the next day they intended to try and reach the summit. It had been in view before them and only about a mile away in a straight line, and in that transparent air must have seemed nearer still. And it might be supposed that men of such ardent nature as Mallory and Somervell would have been in abounding spirits. But Mallory records that that morning there was no exuberance of spirits in the party. We may conclude then that spirits do not exuberate at 25,000 feet. The fact is they were in the exhausted, breathless condition of a runner at the end of a long race. If there had been a crowd present wildly cheering them on, or if they were thought-readers and could read the minds of those at home who were so keenly watching their progress in imagination, they might have felt some elation. As it was, they had to struggle to their goal in death-like silence. In the chill solitude of that highest height the human spirit had to fight its way uncheered.

Snow was falling on the morning of the 21st and a thick mist covered the mountain. Getting into frozen boots and making something hot for breakfast occupied time, and a start was not made till eight. Then the climbers went straight up the mountain, meaning to strike the North-East Ridge – the same ridge that can be seen from Darjiling and Khamba Dzong and which is familiar to us from every photograph of Mount Everest – and work along that. They had hardly made a start when Morshead said he had better not go on: he was feeling done and would not wish to hamper them. So he went back to the tent and awaited their return.

The ascent continued to be steep though not difficult. It was possible to climb almost anywhere on those broken slopes, and there was no question of gymnastic struggles or strong armpulls: they were not climbing a ridge but a face. They were on the face of Everest, though at the edge of it. The real impediment was the difficulty of breathing. They had to avoid hasty, jerky movement and move rhythmically; and, exhausted as they were, they must keep their form and be balanced in their action. Also, they must deliberately take long, deep breaths. They had to breathe through their mouths and not their noses, and the power to breathe in sufficient air – and therefore oxygen – depended on the power of their lungs. These, therefore, they must work methodically.

Proceeding thus they were able to keep moving for from twenty to thirty minutes at a time with rests of three or four minutes. But the difficulty of breathing was telling its tale: they were not moving fast enough; they were making only 400 feet an hour. As they climbed higher they would be making even less. And slowly they became aware that they could not hope to reach the summit. It was 4000 feet from their camp and at their present rate it would take at least ten hours to reach it. Besides, they must keep enough time and energy in reserve to enable them to conduct their return in safety, for comparatively easy as the mountain is, no liberties can be taken with it. These considerations began to have their weight. Their goal was clearly beyond them; and at 2.30 they decided to turn back.

They had reached a point which was afterwards determined by theodolite observations to be 26,985 feet above sea level.

Now when they had attained such a height, 2600 feet higher than anyone had climbed before, it might be supposed that they would be elated. And when they were only three or four hundred feet from the top of the North-East Ridge it might be thought that anyhow they would be eager to push on there, and have a look down the other side and perhaps see the Darjiling ridge. And, at all events, one would think they would feel a thrill at looking down on such a giant as Cho Uyo, not two hundred feet less than 27,000 feet high. But Mallory and his companions had none of these sensations. Feeling was exhausted within them. They accepted the fact that they could not reach the summit. And that being accepted, they turned downwards with some degree of secret satisfaction. Somervell has even admitted that at that moment he did not care a bit whether he got to the top or not. Every spring of effort or enjoyment was exhausted within them.

By four o'clock they were back at the tent and found Morshead cheerful but by no means well, and he had to be carefully treated as they continued their descent to the North Col. And soon was to come an alarming experience which was to show them that even the 'easy' way up Everest had its dangers. The four were roped together, Mallory leading, when the third man slipped, pulling the fourth off his balance. The second man was able to check, but could not quite hold, the last two. And in a moment the three were slipping down the steep slope of the east edge. They were gathering speed and would soon be hurtled to destruction two or three thousand feet below, when Mallory, hearing something wrong behind, instinctively and instantly stuck his ice axe into the snow, hitched the rope round the head of it and leant hard against it. The check the second man had given prevented a sudden strain. The ice axe and the rope held. And the three men's lives were saved. Saved, thanks to Mallory's superb skill as a mountaineer.

This, however, was not to be their last disagreeable experience. After the accident they had to descend a snow slope in which steps had to be cut – always exhausting work – and Morshead was now so ill that he had to be supported. Darkness was gathering. They had still a long way to go and progress was very, very slow as they groped their way down the snow with just the bare outline of rocks to guide them after nightfall. At last they reached the North Col, but they still had to find their way through the tall blocks of ice and amid crevasses. And this was not easy, for even with the light of a lantern they pursued many wrong lines. And not till 11.30 p.m. did they reach the tents where they had supposed their troubles would be over and they would find food, and above all drink – something warm to drink, for they were parched with that thirst which comes to all Everest men from having to inhale such vast quantities of cold dry air. What, then, was their horror when they found that there were not the cooking pots to melt the snow. Through some inadvertence they had been taken back to Camp III. Nothing warm whatever was to be had. And when they were in an agony of thirst the most liquid form of refreshment they could obtain was strawberry jam beaten up with frozen tinned milk and snow.

With nothing more than this to reinforce them after having made the record climb they had to turn in to their sleeping bags, exhausted and worn-out men. It is not surprising that Norton made a mental note that on the next expedition there should be a supporting party at the North Col, with men ready to welcome and assist returning climbers into the camp and supply them immediately with warm drinks and food. Experience teaches much and teaches it sharply.

The descent on the following morning, May 22nd, to Camp III had still to be made; and it was not easy. Much snow had fallen. The old tracks had disappeared. And not only had a new track to be found but steps had to be cut to make it safe for the porters who would have to go up to the North Col camp to bring down the sleeping bags.

It was a thoroughly played-out party that at last arrived at Camp III about noon after starting at six. However, Wakefield then took them in charge. Inexhaustible quantities of tea were made available. And they gradually recovered their spirits. But Morshead's fingers were badly frostbitten, and for months it was a question whether he would retain them.

Chapter Twelve

THE OXYGEN ATTEMPT

As Mallory and his party were descending from the North Col they met Finch coming up to make his climb with oxygen. He was the great enthusiast for its use. Being a lecturer in chemistry he had all the scientific man's keenness for the application of science. And he did with great thoroughness, and minute attention to detail, whatever he took up. He had from the first advocated the use of oxygen and had been put in charge of all pertaining to it from the time its use had been decided on in England.

Oxygen is in constant use by airmen. But till now no attempt had been made by mountaineers to use it on the scale which would be required on Everest. And no apparatus had therefore been previously devised for the purposes of mountaineering. That which the expedition now had was invented for the occasion. It was bound therefore to show defects as it came to be used. And Finch spent much of his time in remedying those defects, as well as in training climbers in its use. This training must have been a thankless task, for no sane man could grow enthusiastic over carrying the cumbersome apparatus and being suffocated by the horrible face piece which was at first supplied. But of course Finch was a fanatic – as every one must be who wants to push a new idea through.

The determination of the man, both as an oxygen enthusiast and as a mountaineer, was invincible. Probably he was not internally really fit when he left England. And in Tibet he had developed bad stomach trouble. However, his will in some fashion managed to reduce his stomach to the peace establishment and on May 16th he left the Base Camp. It had been originally intended that Norton should pair with Finch for the oxygen attempt, but owing to Finch's indisposition Norton had gone on with Morshead to join Mallory and Somervell. Finch, therefore, took with him Geoffrey Bruce.

Geoffrey Bruce in the Alpine Club sense was not a mountaineer. He was only a 'walker'. But he was a remarkably fine walker, and of the build of a climber – tall and slim and not too stocky and thick-set. It is hardly necessary to say that he had also a fine spirit, for that was a common attribute of the whole expedition. He had, too, a certain pliability of mind and readiness to learn, both about mountaineering and the use of oxygen, which is the next best thing to actual experience.

A third member of the oxygen party was the gallant little Gurkha, Lance-Corporal Tejbir, who was to carry reserve cylinders to the highest possible point so that the actual climbers might be able to go further still. He had to play the part of drudge for others who would reap the glory. It is inevitable that some should do this on an expedition. And none were more appreciative of what they owed to these drudges than the glory-reapers themselves.

Wakefield might have been of the party if he had not been feeling these high altitudes more than was expected. He was not so young as he was when he made his famous climbs in Cumberland, and he had to content himself now with the role of advanced base medical officer, accompanying Finch and Geoffrey Bruce to Camp III to give them a final inspection and pass them fit for the high climb.

On the way up the glacier Geoffrey Bruce and Tejbir were given instruction in ice craft and the art of mountaineering; and on May 19th they arrived at Camp III. It was the day that Mallory's party had gone up to the North Col. More amendment and improvement of the oxygen apparatus, and especially of the mouthpiece for inhaling it, had here to be made. On May 22nd Finch and party went up to meet and succour Mallory's party on the North Col, and also to make a final test of the apparatus. They succeeded in reaching the Col in good time and returning the same afternoon to Camp III. They went up in three hours and down in fifty minutes, and Finch was well satisfied with the results.

And now they were joined by Noel. Noel was only the photographer and only a 'walker', but he was as set and keen on the idea of climbing Everest as anyone in the expedition. It had been his own idea for years. He was a man of deep intensity of nature and of fine feeling for mountain beauty. His ambition was to make a perfect record of the expedition in both still and moving photographs. He wanted to catch and express the spirit of the mountains, the awe they inspire, their terrible character, their might and their glory, and withal their irresistible attraction. He had the artist strongly in him. And he was also a man of untiring industry. Every member of the expedition said on its return that Noel worked harder than anyone. For when he was not out on the mountain side taking his photographs he was spending hours developing them in his tent – and developing them under trying conditions, for the constant and tearing wind brought dust or powdery snow everywhere and the cold immediately froze water or any solution. Another drawback to photography in this region was the excessive dryness. As the cinematograph instrument was being turned, little sparks of electricity were given off which blurred the impression.

To take Noel and his cinematograph high up on Everest was more than could be managed with the porterage available. The North Col was, however, within range, and he therefore accompanied Finch and Geoffrey Bruce as they set out on May 24th for what may be called the oxygen assault on the mountain. That night they spent at the North Col camp, and leaving Noel there Finch and party started off up the mountain on May 25th.

Twelve porters carrying oxygen cylinders, provisions for one day, and camping gear, accompanied Finch, Bruce and Tejbir, the porters starting first and the climbers one and a half hours later. These latter were carrying a load of over thirty pounds each, for such is the weight of the oxygen apparatus, but through being able to reinforce themselves by inhaling oxygen they overtook the porters at about 24,500 feet and pressed on, hoping to pitch a camp at about 26,000 feet. This proved, however, to be impossible; for at about one o'clock the wind freshened and snow fell, the weather generally began to look threatening, and a site for a camp had to be sought for at once, as the porters would have to return to the North Col and their lives must not be endangered through having to descend in a blizzard.

The altitude at which the party now stood was 25,500 feet. It was lower than the climbers had aimed at reaching, and even that was further than advisable from the summit; it still left

3000 feet to be climbed, and so big a climb might not be possible. But, no more being possible that day, a little platform was built up on the spot selected, the tent was pitched on it, and the porters were dispatched back to the North Col.

It was a precarious position in which Finch, Bruce and Tejbir were placed. They were hanging on to the mountain slopes by the tips of their fingers, as it were. They were not firmly placed on solid ground: they were propped up on a slope. They were on the very edge of the tremendous precipices which fell away to the Rongbuk glaciers 4000 feet below. A tempest was brewing, and it was snowing hard – and the fine, powdery snow driven by the wind penetrated the tent and permeated everything inside. It was bitterly cold, too, and the three, huddled together inside their little tentlet, tried to warm themselves with hot drinks from melted snow. And even that was not very comforting, for at these high altitudes water boils at so low a temperature that a really hot drink cannot be had. Nothing more than tepid tea or soup can be concocted.

After sunset the tempest was on them in its full fury. It tore at the fragile little tent, and threatened to sweep it and its human contents ignominiously off the mountain. Frequently, the men had to go out into the swirling blizzard and tighten the guy ropes and pile on more stones. All through the night the struggle with the elements had to be maintained without slackening. Sleep was out of the question, both on account of the wild flapping of the tent and also because of the need of constant vigilance lest they should be hurled down the precipice. And always this spindrift was being driven hard through tent and bedding and clothing and causing acutest discomfort.

At daybreak the snow had ceased but the wind was as violent

as ever. There could be no hope of starting up the mountain – yet, at any rate. Or even of starting down. They must remain where they were. By noon the fury of the storm increased still further and a stone cut a hole in the tent which made the situation still worse. Then, at one o'clock, the wind dropped suddenly to the level of a strong breeze, and the chance offered itself of making a dash back to safety at the North Col.

If 'safety first' had been the rule this would have been the course to take. But the indomitable spirit of the climbers was not yet overcome. They still clung to the hope of renewing their upward climb on the following day. And before evening cheering reinforcement arrived. Voices were heard outside the tent, and porters appeared sent up by Noel from the North Col with thermos flasks of hot beef-tea and tea.

And this little incident in itself is another illustration of how the standard of achievement was rising. Men being sent with thermos flasks to 25,500 feet! And on a nasty day, too; and with night coming on! And the loyalty of the men who did it! Wonderful is it how much follows on quite naturally from strenuously striving for the highest!

The climbers gratefully took in the flasks and sent the porters back to the North Col. But they were now much exhausted. The want of sleep and the constant effort required in keeping the tent secure had told hardly upon them. And thus weakened, the cold was having its effect. A dead, numbing feeling was creeping up their limbs. And in this extremity they bethought themselves of the oxygen. They took doses all round and warmth began to tingle through them again. Through the night they continued to take these doses at intervals, and owing to this refreshment they were able to get a tolerable amount of sleep.

Before daybreak they were up preparing for the climb. Boots were frozen solid and an hour was occupied in moulding them into shape by holding them over candles. At 6.30 they started, Finch and Bruce with the oxygen apparatus, cameras, thermos bottles, etc., carrying well over 40 lb, and Tejbir with two extra cylinders carrying about 50 lb. It was a cruel burden for men to have to carry; and the faith which could have induced men to do this should have sufficed to remove Everest itself. Whether that faith was justified is another question.

Finch's intention was to strike on up the face edge to the ridge. Tejbir with his spare cylinders was to be taken as far as the ridge and then to be sent back to the tent to await Finch's and Bruce's return. But the load was too much for poor Tejbir, and before they had gone more than a few hundred feet he collapsed. All Bruce's persuasion could not induce him to go further. So he had to be sent back. It is indeed a marvel that he had done so much. And all honour is due – and was given him – for his fine deed. He had reached an altitude of nearly 26,000 feet.

The remaining two now proceeded on, and as the climbing was easy they dispensed with the rope. They passed two almost level places which would afford ample room for a camp and gained an altitude of 26,500 feet. And then the wind became so strong that Finch thought it necessary to discontinue the ascent of the face edge and to strike out right across the face itself. By so doing he hoped to find more shelter from the icy blasts which he expected he would experience on the actual ridge.

But the going was not so good on the face itself as it had been on the edge. The general angle became much steeper and the stratification of the rocks was such that they shelved outward and downward. And sometimes the slabs gave place to treacherous powdery snow with a thin, hard, deceptive crust that gave the appearance of compactness. Foothold in these circumstances was not always secure. But Finch, in order to save time, still did not use the rope: he and Bruce climbed across the face independently.

Since leaving the face edge they had not been rising much as they were moving in a nearly horizontal direction. But they were getting nearer the summit in point of distance, and this was cheering. And at 27,000 feet they struck diagonally upwards towards a point on the ridge about halfway along it in the direction of the summit, till an accident put Bruce's oxygen apparatus out of action. Finch linked Bruce's up with his own so that he might still inhale oxygen, and then traced the trouble and effected a satisfactory repair.

'Traced the trouble and effected a satisfactory repair'. This in itself was a feat; for men's faculties at an altitude of 27,300 feet are numbed almost to extinction. Climbers can barely plod dully, mechanically on, their brains like wool. But Finch did still retain some alertness of mind, as well as strength of will, and so was able to repair the apparatus.

They had, however, gone far enough. They were weak from hunger and exhausted by that night's struggle with the wind. They were still too far from the summit for there to be the slightest chance of reaching it. They were perhaps only half a mile from it, but they were a good seventeen hundred feet below. There was no object in straining further; they could only go back: hard facts were against them.

At this culminating point of their effort they were right out on the Face of Everest at a height of 27,235 feet. What did they see? And what did they feel? Again there is little record, and for the simple reason that what little remained of activity in their minds had to be devoted to the task immediately before them of getting up and down the mountain. The most that Finch can say is that there was much cloud about and that Pumori – Pumori, that beautiful mountain, 23,000 feet in height – could hardly be seen at first; it had sunk into an insignificant little ice hump by the side of the Rongbuk Glacier. He could not remember even to take a photograph, though he had a camera with him. All their thoughts were directed to getting down again.

And having decided to return, Finch and Bruce quickly started off downward, now roped together in case any accidental interruption in the oxygen supply might lead to a slip by one or other. Progress was more rapid, though caution was necessary. About 2 p.m. they struck the face edge again and there dumped four of their cylinders, and in barely half an hour reached their tent, where they found Tejbir snugly wrapped in all three sleeping bags and sleeping the deep sleep of exhaustion. Porters were now seen ascending to bring the kit down, and Finch and Bruce, leaving Tejbir to them, pressed on to the North Col. They felt weak and shaky and just staggered along, but managed to reach the North Col camp at four o'clock. Here Noel had hot tea and a tin of spaghetti ready for them. And three-quarters of an hour later, feeling strong and refreshed, they started on again, Noel accompanying them and nursing them safely down the steep snow and ice slopes on to the almost level basin of the glacier below. By 5.30 p.m. they were at Camp III, having descended 6000 feet from their highest point.

The attempt to reach the summit had failed. But this oxygen climb was a prodigious effort – an exhibition of cold, inflexible determination which could scarcely be surpassed.

Chapter Thirteen

AN AVALANCHE

Another great feat of mountaineering had been performed, another record established; but Everest was still unconquered. That was the brutal fact that had now to be faced. Everest was still unconquered and the expedition was almost exhausted. There were no reserves available. The best mountaineers had already made their effort. And men can hardly make two efforts on Everest in the same season. Still the climbers were not even yet prepared to accept defeat. They would go on till they were definitely turned back. This was their attitude as they lay at the Base Camp recuperating.

Somervell was on the whole the fittest. Mallory was suffering from a slight frostbite, and his heart was to a small extent affected. Norton also was frostbitten and weakened in the heart. And Morshead was in constant pain from frostbite and there was great risk of his losing his fingers. These two last would certainly have to go back without any possible delay to Sikkim. And when Finch and Geoffrey Bruce arrived at the Base Camp it was found that the latter's feet were so badly frostbitten that he could not walk. Finch himself, though greatly exhausted, was not affected by frostbite or in the heart.

This was the not very hopeful condition of the climbers at the end of May. Strutt, too, was very much overdone. Longstaff was not his old self. And neither Wakefield nor Crawford had acclimatized well for high altitudes.

But there might be just time before the monsoon broke to make one more effort if a few of these recovered a little more. Strutt, Morshead, Geoffrey Bruce, Norton and Longstaff would certainly have to go down to Sikkim at once. There was just a chance, though, that Mallory's heart might improve and Finch recover from his exhaustion.

On June 3rd Mallory was examined and found to be fit, and it was at once arranged that a third attempt should be made, though General Bruce warned all concerned that they were to run no undue risks with the monsoon. Mallory, Somervell and Finch would constitute the climbing party, Wakefield and Crawford furnish the support at Camp III. And plenty of porters would be available for both. That same day the party reached Camp I, but Finch was so obviously unfit to proceed that he went back the next day and joined Longstaff's party of invalids on their way to Sikkim. He had indeed done his full share already and no one could expect him to do more. And this day, June 4th, showed ominous signs of the monsoon. Snow was falling heavily and the party had to remain where they were. They might well have gone back, recognizing that the monsoon had broken and acknowledging that no further attempt was possible. But the break of the monsoon in that region is no very definite occurrence. Heavy snow falls and then there is a pause and a spell of fine weather. It was on the chance of a spell of fine weather that Mallory counted. They would not, he writes, run their heads into obvious dangers; but, rather than be stopped by a general estimate of conditions, they would prefer to retire before some definite risk that they were not prepared to take, or simply fail to overcome the difficulties.

Snow fell all the second night at Camp I, but on the morning of June 5th the weather improved and they decided to go on. They were surprised to find that this fall of snow had made little difference on the glacier. Most of it had melted or evaporated and it lay only six inches deep. So they passed Camp II and proceeded straight on to Camp III. And here the snow was much deeper and the whole scene, with the clouds hanging about the mountain side, grey and cheerless. Moreover, the tents had been struck in order to save the poles and were now half full of snow and ice; and the stores were buried in the snow and had to be dug out.

Was it possible under these circumstances to go on? Was there really any prospect of their reaching the summit or climbing any higher than they had already climbed? That evening it seemed doubtful. But the next morning broke fine; there was soon a clear sky and glorious sunshine; and hope revived, especially as snow was being blown from the North-East Ridge and it would soon be fit to climb.

And now they were pinning their faith on the oxygen. They would not be able to establish a second camp above the North Col. And without a second camp they knew they could not, unaided, climb higher than where they had already reached. But oxygen was to work wonders. Somervell had learnt about the mechanical details from Finch, so could manage the apparatus, he was sure. And those who had used the oxygen were so convinced of its efficacy that Mallory and Somervell made themselves believe in it too. They intended to profit by

Finch's experience. They would again try to pitch a camp at 26,000 feet. And they would not begin using oxygen until they had reached 25,000 feet.

The wall to the North Col, however, had first to be tackled. They did not expect to reach the Col in one day: the amount of new snow on it was too great. But they could begin work at once carrying loads up some part of the way, for they must make the most of the fine weather while it lasted. That same day, therefore, June 7th, they commenced this work.

They started at 8 a.m. and, in spite of the hard frost during the night, they found the crust hardly bore their weight and they sank up to their knees at almost every step. Avalanches they might expect, but they feared them only in one place, the steep final 200-feet slope below the shelf on which Camp IV was pitched. There they would have to proceed with caution, testing the snow before they crossed the slope. For the rest of the way they thought there would be no danger.

Wakefield had been left at Camp III as supply officer, and the party on this North Col wall now consisted of Mallory, Somervell, and Crawford, with fourteen porters. It was clear that the three climbers, having no loads, must take the lead, stamping out a track for the laden porters as they ascended the steep ice slope, now covered with snow. This snow adhered so well to the ice that they were able to get up without cutting steps. Everything was done by trenching the snow to induce it to come down if it would. But there was no move. And this crucial place being passed they plodded on without hesitation. If snow would not come down there, it would not come down on the gentler slopes, they believed. There was no risk now of an avalanche.

So they struggled on through the deep snow; and exhausting work it was, as after each lifting movement it was necessary to pause for a whole series of breaths before the weight was transferred again to the other foot. Fortunately, the day was bright and windless; and by 1.30 they were about 400 feet below a conspicuous block of ice and 600 feet below the North Col, still on the gentle slopes of the corridor. Here they rested for a time till the porters, following on three separate ropes, came up. Then the whole party advanced again, carefully indeed but unsuspicious of danger.

They had proceeded only 100 feet, Somervell leading, and rather up the slope than across it, and the last party of porters had barely begun to move up in his steps, when all of a sudden they were startled by 'an ominous sound, sharp, arresting, violent and yet somehow soft like an explosion of untamped gun-powder'. Mallory had never before heard such a sound. But he knew instinctively what it meant. He observed the surface of the snow break and pucker. Then he was borne slowly downward in the moving surface, carried along by an irresistible force. He managed to turn out from the slope so as to avoid being pushed headlong and backwards down it. And for a second or two he seemed hardly to be in danger as he went quietly sliding down with the snow. Then the rope at his waist tightened and held him back. A wave of snow came over him and he was buried. All seemed to be up with him. But he remembered that the best chance of escape in such a situation was by swimming. So he thrust out his arm over his head and went through the motions of swimming on his back. Then he felt the pace of the avalanche easing up. At length it came to rest. His arms were free. His legs were near the surface. And after a brief struggle he was standing, surprised and breathless, in the motionless snow.

But the rope was tight at his waist: the porter tied on next to him, he supposed, must be deeply buried. To Mallory's surprise he emerged, unharmed. Somervell and Crawford also soon extricated themselves. Their experiences had been much the same as Mallory's.

So far so good. And one group of four porters could be seen 150 feet below. Perhaps the others would be safe too. But these four were pointing downward, and it was evident that the other porters must have been carried further. Mallory and his companions hurried to them and they soon saw that beneath the place where the four porters were standing was a formidable drop – an ice cliff 40 feet high. The missing men must have been swept over it. The climbers quickly found a way round to its base, and then their worst fears were confirmed. One man was rapidly disinterred and found to be still alive; and he recovered. Another, carrying four oxygen cylinders on a steel frame, and found upside down, was still breathing, though he had been buried for about forty minutes. And he also recovered, and was able to walk down to Camp III. But seven were killed.

Thus the third attempt ended in a tragedy. Evidently the party ought not to have ventured on the North Col slopes. But to say that is only to be wise after the event. To all appearances the conditions were safe. And Mallory and Somervell were experienced – and cautious – mountaineers. They were working against time, it may be admitted. But they were not the men to run needless risks; and they were not the men to risk the lives of their poor laden porters unnecessarily. For these porters they had, indeed, the greatest respect and affection.

The effect of the loss upon the British members of the expedition was one of deep compassion for men who had lost their lives in faithfully playing their part in a great adventure. The effect upon the relatives and friends of these men and upon the peoples round has been described by General Bruce in some passages of his report which are particularly valuable as showing the attitude of local peoples to accidents of this kind.

On receipt of the news he communicated it to the great lama of the Rongbuk Monastery, who was 'intensely sympathetic and kind over the whole matter'. Buddhist services were held in the monasteries for the men who were killed and for their families. And all the porters, and particularly the relations of the men who were killed, were received and specially blessed by the lama himself. Later on General Bruce also received from his friend the Maharaja of Nepal a letter of condolence. 'This puts in my mind', His Highness wrote, 'the curious belief that persistently prevails with the people here, and which I came to learn so long ago in the time of our mutual friend, Colonel Manners Smith, when the question of giving permission for the project of climbing the King of Heights through Nepal was brought by you and discussed in a council of Bharadars. It is to the effect that the height is the abode of the god and goddess Shiva and Parvati, and any invasion of the privacy of it would be a sacrilege fraught with disastrous consequences to the Hindu country and its people. And this belief or superstition, as one may choose to call it, is so firm and strong that people attribute the present tragic occurrence to the divine wrath which on no account would they draw on their heads by any action.'

Thus was the calamity viewed by the Tibetans on the north and the Nepalese on the south of Everest. Bruce says of the Tibetans that they are a curious mixture of superstition and nice feelings. And the same he would evidently say of the Nepalese.

He further says that the Nepalese tribes who live high up in the mountains, and also the Sherpa Bhutias, have a belief that when a man slips and is killed this is a sacrifice to God, and especially to the god of the actual mountain. They further believe that anyone who happens to be on the same mountain at the same place, at the same date and hour, will also slip and be killed.

However, notwithstanding this calamity and these super-stitions, the remaining porters of the expedition soon took a light-hearted view of things. They held simply that the men's time had come. If their time had not come they would not have died. It had come and they had died. There was no need to say more. That was their fatalistic creed. And they were perfectly ready to join another Everest expedition. If it was written they would die on Everest they would die. If it was written that they would not die they wouldn't. There was an end of the matter.

The calamity did not therefore in the least discourage them or others. And they and their fellows came forward just as readily for the next as they had for this expedition.

Nevertheless, the climbers themselves were deeply con-cerned at the disaster. They felt it as a slur on their character as mountaineers. But, if slur it was, Mallory and Somervell amply removed it two years later on this very same spot, as we shall presently hear.

Chapter Fourteen

HIGH-ALTITUDE LIFE

The summit had not been attained; but man had of his own strength climbed to 27,000 feet above sea level. *Has any other living thing done the same?* Has any other animal, or any insect, or even any bird, reached that stupendous height? It may be doubted. A chough did, two years later, accompany another climbing party to that same altitude to gather scraps of their food. But choughs do not fly to that height either for the view or for the glory of the thing. And this was the first time in the history of the world that food had been carried to 27,000 feet on a mountain. We may assume then that no chough had been to that height before. Vultures soar to great heights, and Wollaston in 1921 had observed a vulture sailing over the North Peak at about 25,000 feet. But it was not 2000 feet above it. And this is the highest known altitude at which vultures have been seen. They would not rise higher than they need; and there is no obvious need for them to fly as high as 27,000 feet.

So far then as is known, man, in 1922, attained a higher height than any living thing had reached on his own power. He had on his legs risen higher than the winged creatures.

And these Everest expeditions have afforded an excellent

opportunity of learning how high various creatures do rise. The question was more particularly examined by the naturalist of the next expedition, Major Hingston, Indian Medical Service. But all three expeditions contributed to the knowledge, and this is a convenient place in which to recount the results.

The highest permanent inhabitants of the earth appear to be some spiders which Major Hingston found at an altitude of 22,000 feet. They were little Attid spiders, immature, minute, black in colour. They lived among rocky debris, lurking in fissures and hiding beneath stones. What they feed on is a mystery, for at that height there is nothing but bare rock and ice – no plant life whatever or any other visible form of organic life. Bees, butterflies and moths may occasionally be *blown* to these altitudes, but this seems to be the natural *home* of these spiders: they are inhabitants, not migrants.

The highest plant seen was a small arenaria (*A. musciformis*) which Wollaston found growing in flat cushions, a few inches wide, up to 20,100 feet. He also found a few grasses and mosses and edelweiss at 20,000 feet.

These were the highest residents. Among visitors, besides the lammergeier vulture which Wollaston saw flying at 25,000 feet and the chough which accompanied a 1924 party to 27,000 feet, Somervell saw choughs around the summit of Kharta Phu at 23,640 feet. Tracks seen in the snow at 21,500 feet were almost certainly the tracks of a wolf, and wolves themselves were seen at about 19,000 feet. Wollaston twice saw a hoopoe fly over the Kharta Glacier at about 21,000 feet. A small pale hawk flew overhead at about the same time.

At Camp III, 21,000 feet, Hingston saw choughs and a jungle crow, both of which seem to have followed up the camp.

COLONEL NORTON AT 28,000 FEET.

THE ABBOT OF SHEKAR CHÖTE.

The Kama Valley.

CLIFFS OF CHOMOLÖNZO FROM CAMP AT PETHANG RINGMO.

NORTH COL.

Base Camp and Mount Everest in evening light.

Seracs, East Rongbuk Glacier, above Camp II.

Camp IV
(on this ledge)

THE ROUTE TO THE NORTH COL.

NORTH COL AND NORTH-EAST SHOULDER OF MOUNT EVEREST.

Mallory and Norton.

MORSHEAD MALLORY SOMERVELL NORTON

THE FIRST CLIMBING PARTY.

CAMP No. II.

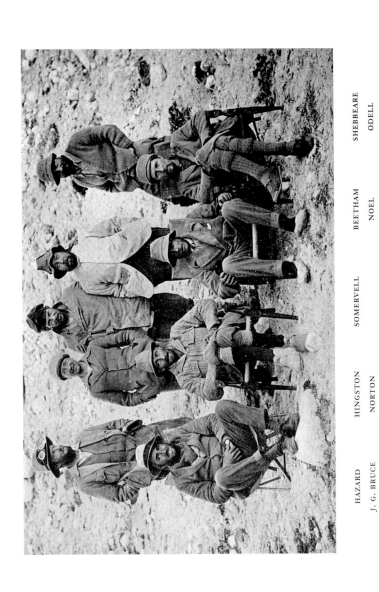

HAZARD   HINGSTON   SOMERVELL   BEETHAM   SHEBBEARE
J. G. BRUCE   NORTON   NOEL   ODELL

MEMBERS OF THE EXPEDITION, 1924.

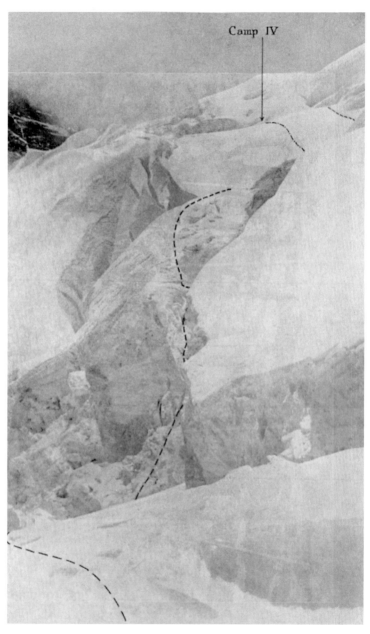

ROUTE UP THE CHIMNEY.

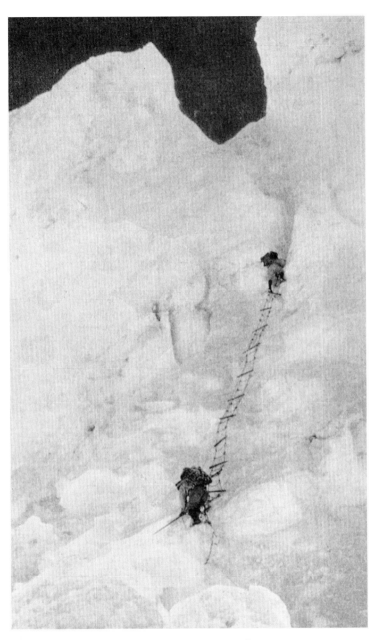

THE CHIMNEY, NORTH COL.

BOM NAPBOO VISHAV SEMCHUMBI LOBSANG LHAKPA CHEDI ANGTENJIN

PORTERS WHO WENT HIGHEST.

And a rose-finch which he saw there seemed to have been migrating across the range. Another visitor was a humble-bee. Traces of fox and hare were seen by Wollaston at 21,000 and they were both seen above 20,000 feet.

The camp at 20,000 feet on the Kharta Glacier was daily visited by lammergeier, raven, red-billed chough, alpine chough, and black-eared kite. Droppings of burrhel were seen at 20,000, and the sheep themselves were fairly common between 17,000 feet and 19,000 feet. A pika of a new species (*Ochotona wollastoni*) was found from 15,000 feet to 20,000 feet. An unseen mouse entered the tents and ate food at 20,000 feet.

At 19,000 feet in the Kharta Valley dwarf blue meconopsis, many saxifrages and curious sasusureas, large composites packed with cottonwool, were found.

At 18,000 feet were the smallest rhododendrons (*R. Setosum* and *R. Zepidotum*), a dwarf blue hairy delphinium (*D. brunnoneanum*) in the Kharta Valley; and Wollaston also saw there at this altitude the very handsome red-breasted rose-finch. And Hingston found immature forms of a new genus of grasshopper on the desolate moraines at 18,000 feet, and at the same height was a Guldenstadt's redstart.

Descending to 17,000 feet life becomes much more numerous. In the Kharta Valley growing along the edges of the streams was a very handsome gentian (*G. nubigena*) with half a dozen flowers growing on a single stem; and near by was an aromatic little purple and yellow aster (*A. heterochoeta*) and a bright yellow senecio (*S. arnicoides*) with shiny glossy leaves. A curious dark blue dead-nettle (*Dracocephalum speciosum*) grew on dry ground. He also mentions seeing the beautiful *Gentiana ornata*, but whether as high as this is not clear.

At this altitude man appears. Hingston relates that a solitary hermit had imprisoned himself in a cell at 17,000 feet in the Rongbuk Valley. Robber-flies, hunting-wasps, the Tibetan hare, a mouse-hare, and tortoiseshell and Apollo butterflies he also saw at this height, and herds of burrhel worked along the hill side.

Birds of several species were seen by Wollaston at this height in the Kharta Valley. The Tibetan snow partridge (*Tetraogallus tibetanus*) were common in large parties up to the snow line. Dippers (*Cinclus cashmiriensis*) were found in the streams, and in the big boulders of moraines was a small and very dark wren. Snow-finches and the Eastern alpine accentor appeared to be resident up to the snow line. And several migrating birds were seen in September at 17,000 feet and above, among them Temminck's stint, painted snipe, pintailed snipe, house martin and several pipits. More than once at night migrating waders were heard, curlew being unmistakable.

At 16,000 feet was the Rongbuk Monastery. And at the Base Camp Hingston saw mountain finches, the brown accentor, the wallcreeper, ravens, lammergeiers, hill pigeons and choughs. Adams' mountain finch and Guldenstadt's redstart nested at this altitude. Dung beetles were found in every pad of dung and beneath the carcass of every dead animal. A rare little wasp was wont to work in clay here. Bugs were found; and ticks sheltered beneath stones.

We have now reached the level of the summit of Mont Blanc and need not pursue the subject further. But we may note how great a variety of life exists at an altitude higher than the summit of the highest mountain in Europe. Animals will ascend the mountain side as far as their accustomed food supply is obtainable, says Hingston, and they are not deterred by physical inclemence. They will brave the cold wind and the rarefied atmosphere provided that a suitable supply of food can be secured. He believes that if a camp were established on the top of Everest choughs would follow it there.

Chapter Fifteen

THE CHIEF RESULT

Everest had not been climbed and another expedition would be necessary. But what experience had this expedition gained that would be of service to the next?

It had made a discovery of outstanding importance – and of importance not only for future Everest expeditions but for mankind generally. It had discovered that man acclimatizes himself to the effects of the highest altitudes. Man adapts himself to breathing thinner and thinner air and to the lessening quantity of oxygen in it found at higher and higher altitudes. If the spirit of man – his love of adventure, his pride in himself, his joy in exerting himself to the fullest and showing himself off to his fellows, and his love of their approbation and praise and encouragement – will drive him on to climbing the highest heights, he will find himself rising to the occasion; he will find both body and mind responding to the call of the spirit.

This is the discovery that the second Everest expedition made and, as we shall see, it was confirmed in the fullest degree by the third. And the significance of this discovery we shall understand if we recall the opinions of scientific men before these expeditions set out. It had then been thought that acclimatization would be impossible above the altitude of 20,000 feet. That is to say, if you climbed from 20,000 to 23,000 feet twice, you would feel the effects of altitude (as apart from physical exhaustion) more the second time than you did the first. And if you climbed to 23,000 feet a third time you would feel worse still. Similarly, if you remained at 23,000 feet two days you would feel worse on the second day than on the first. And if you remained three days you would feel worse still. You would have exceeded the limit of acclimatization. You would no longer adapt yourself to the changed conditions in which you found yourself. You would be unable to respond to the call your spirit was making upon you. Instead of rising to the occasion you would lie down under it. You would have to acknowledge defeat by your material surroundings instead of having the joy of defeating them.

This was the gloomy outlook of many scientists before the expedition. And it all came of their lack of faith in themselves. They were full of faith in their science, but for some mysterious reason they were always concentrating their attention on the physics and chemistry and mechanics of the world, and on microbes and diseases, and paying small attention to man himself, and man as a whole – and when they studied man at all it was mostly his body they paid attention to, and to his body when it was ill. They dealt with tiny abstractions of man and abstractions of the world. They did not deal with wholes. Consequently they came to wrong conclusions.

For the Everest expedition discovered that if man's spirit drove him up to 23,000 feet a second time he felt the effects of altitude *less* on the second occasion than on the first. This test by actual human experiment was repeated over and over again and at higher altitudes than 23,000, and it always gave the same result. And the expedition was fortunate in this, that it had a medical man with it who happened to have been connected with physiological research for some years, and who was one of those who climbed highest on Everest – climbed to a height of practically 27,000 feet, and without using oxygen. And he has recorded his experience.

Speaking of the climb to the North Col, 23,000 feet, Somervell says, 'I shall never forget our first ascent up that accursed slope of snow and ice, each step a hardship, every foot a fight: until we at last lay, almost exhausted, on the top.' That was his experience of first climbing to 23,000 feet. Now let us hear what he has to say about his experience on his second climb to 23,000 feet. 'After a day or two at Camp III (21,000 feet) below', he says, 'we went up again to the col. The ascent of the col this time was hard work, but not more than that; and after the col had been reached Morshead and I were sufficiently cheerful to explore the way leading up to Everest.'

So Somervell felt the effects of high altitude *less*, not more, on the second occasion than on the first. And now let us hear what he has to say about his third climb to 23,000 feet. 'A day or two later', he says, 'we again ascended the North Col, and never really noticed more discomfort than was occasioned by breathlessness . . . in those few days of life at 21,000 feet we had become acclimatized to our altitude to a very remarkable degree: what had previously been a hard struggle had now become a comparatively easy job.' Thus Somervell felt the altitude less and less, not more and more. And the experience of others corroborated his own. Here then was evidence that men do acclimatize at least as high as 23,000 feet.

And this adaptation of their constitutions to the effects of high altitude gave Somervell the physical power to enable him to reach 27,000 feet without oxygen. His experience, corroborated by other experiences, proved both the rapidity of acclimatization and its persistence to great heights. Acclimatization is both possible and rapid at high altitudes.

And we may note that this acclimatization is of the mind as well as of the body. The body, without the mind being aware of it, goes through some obscure process of adapting itself to the altered conditions. The number of blood corpuscles is increased and no doubt other changes take place. But the mind also adapts itself. When the climbers and porters first started for the North Col there was uncertainty in their minds as to whether or not they could attain 23,000 feet with any spare energy left for going higher. Once having attained that height the standard of achievement rose in their minds. They eventually came to think little of going to 23,000 feet. Porters went up and down time after time. Noel slept there for three consecutive nights. Mallory and Somervell, Finch and Bruce slept higher still. When the expedition started the camp at 21,000 feet was looked upon as the base for operations. When it came back they regarded the North Col, 23,000 feet, as the starting point. Their minds had risen in the scale of achievement and been acclimatized like their bodies to the higher heights.

But did the expedition get any proof of acclimatization *above* 23,000 feet? Not much. Each of the climbers went only once higher than that. But porters did twice visit the 25,500 feet camp. On the first occasion there was great difficulty in getting them to go as high as that. But on the second occasion they went up quite naturally. Finch and Geoffrey Bruce might be in distress there, so Noel at 23,000 feet calls up a porter or two, says, 'Take these thermos flasks up to Finch Sahib,' and off they go. The wind is dreadful. Night will be on them most likely before they get back. But they deliver the goods all right. And this at an altitude higher by a thousand feet than man till this year had ever reached before.

These experiences led Somervell to think that there was no theoretic limit to acclimatization at any level below the top of Mount Everest. He predicted that acclimatization at 23,000 feet would be sufficient for the attainment of the summit. He believed it would be possible to reach the summit without the use of oxygen. There must be many people, he thought, who could get to the top of Everest unaided save by their own physiological reaction to a life at 21,000 feet for a few days. 'If a number of such people were allowed to live at a height corresponding to Camp III (21,000 feet) for a fortnight or so, making perhaps a few excursions to 23,000 or 24,000 feet, then I have no doubt, from the physiological point of view, that they will be able to climb Mount Everest, provided the weather is fine and the wind not too violent.' He therefore predicted that 'the best chance of getting to the top of Mount Everest lies in the sending out of some nine or ten climbers, who can remain at a high camp, become thoroughly acclimatized, and then make a series of expeditions up the mountain, three or so at a time, as continuously as weather conditions will allow.'

It is a thousand pities that these conclusions were not acted upon. And the present writer includes himself in the blame he thus puts upon those responsible for the organization of the third expedition. But the idea of acclimatization at the highest altitudes has not even now thoroughly got hold of men's minds. And in 1923 they were still obsessed with the idea that oxygen was necessary – and Somervell himself was partly to blame for this as he had so persuasively induced the Mount Everest Committee to equip the 1922 expedition with an oxygen outfit. Oxygen was therefore supplied to the third expedition, as to the second.

The truth is we have not yet sufficiently appreciated that as a race we men are still very young – not more than half a million years old. We are yet in the stage of testing and proving our capacities. We have not finished climbing about our surroundings on this little planet of ours, and seeing what we can do and where we can go. We find it difficult, at present, to clamber up on to the top of Mount Everest, and we tumble back at the first try. But we don't yet know of what we are capable and should take heart from the young of animals and birds as they daringly find their wings or their legs.

If one thing stands out more than another in importance among the results of this – and the next – expedition, it is that man's capacities are still growing, and that if he exercises them they expand. There are plenty of grounds for having more faith in ourselves.

Chapter Sixteen

THE USE OF OXYGEN

There was some excuse for using oxygen. We knew so little, in 1922, about men's capacities for climbing above the 25,000-feet level, it might have proved foolish not to use it when we could. But in the result oxygen has been the bane of Everest expeditions. Finch was its chief advocate in addition to Somervell in the first instance. And the tragedy is that this magnificent mountaineer, with his experience and skill, his absolutely unconquerable will and his sense of the glory to be won by climbing Mount Everest, might have been the very man to reach the top without it. What led him astray was the conviction scientific men had, before these Everest expeditions started, that men would not be able to live in the rare air of the extreme heights. To him, therefore, as a scientific man, it seemed silly not to use oxygen. With oxygen, if some means of carrying it up could be found, it would be certain that the top could be reached. Without oxygen it then seemed almost equally certain that the summit would not be reached. We wanted to reach the summit. The obvious course then was to plump for oxygen. This was his line of thought. He was a scientist. He would apply his science. He would use oxygen.

And, according to his nature, he got his mind so fixed on the idea of using oxygen that he could not drag himself from it, even when it was found that men acclimatize rapidly as high as 23,000 feet.

The expedition had taught him not the value of acclimatization but the value of oxygen. And he fortified himself in this conclusion by comparing the results of the two high climbs – the one without oxygen on May 22nd, and the other with oxygen on May 27th. 'After over six hours' climbing', he says, 'Mallory, Norton, and Somervell succeeded in reaching an altitude of 26,985 feet; so that since their departure from their high camp, they had gained a vertical height of 1985 feet at a rate of ascent of 330 feet per hour. The point at which they turned back . . . is, in horizontal distance, about 1⅛ miles from the summit, and rather over 2000 feet below it in vertical height. They began to retrace their steps at 2.30 in the afternoon, and regained their high camp at four o'clock; their rate of descent therefore was 1320 feet per hour. Shortly after 4 p.m., accompanied by Morshead, they arrived on the return journey to the North Col, where they arrived at 11.30 that night, a rate of descent of 270 feet per hour.' He then describes how he met them the next morning on their way to Camp III, 'obviously in the last stages of exhaustion'.

Compared with this non-oxygen climb he takes his own oxygen climb. On May 27th at 6 a.m., having had practically no rest for two nights and a day, half starved and suffering acutely from hunger, he and Geoffrey Bruce set out from their camp at 25,500 feet in full hopes of gaining the summit. Half an hour later Tejbir broke down. At 26,500 feet they struck off on to the face of Everest; having climbed the height of a thousand feet from their camp in one and a half hours, that is to say, at a rate of 900 feet per hour, in spite of the fact that they each carried a load of over 40 lb. After this they gained but little in altitude, but steadily approached the summit. Eventually they turned back at a point less than half a mile in horizontal distance from, and about 1700 feet below, the summit. They had climbed in vertical height only some 300 feet higher than the non-oxygen party, nevertheless they were more than twice as close to the summit.

And summarizing the two performances he says: 'The first party established a camp at an altitude of 25,000 feet, occupied it for one night, and finally reaching a point 26,985 feet in height, and 1⅛ miles from the summit, returned without a break to the North Col. The second party established a camp at an altitude of 25,500 feet, occupied it for two nights and almost two days, and eventually reaching a point 27,300 feet high, and less than half a mile from the summit, returned without a break to Camp III.' And he maintains that as regards weather the oxygen party experienced incomparably worse conditions than the first.

He therefore concludes that 'the contention that the dis-advantages of its weight more than counterbalance the advan-tages of an artificial supply of oxygen may be dismissed as groundless.' And he assumes that on any further attempt upon Everest oxygen will form a most important part of the climber's equipment.

Now all this may be perfectly true and it may be granted that climbers could reach the summit of Everest with oxygen if they could get porters enough to carry up not only the tents and supplies but the oxygen cylinders, and if no defects in the oxygen apparatus developed as the highest altitudes were reached. And if there were not the faintest chance of their being able to get up without oxygen, then oxygen certainly should be used. But the point is that the 1922 expedition showed that there *is* a chance of their being able to reach the summit without oxygen; and taking everything into consideration – lack of porters, defects in apparatus and so on – quite as good a chance as with it. And the climbing of Everest without oxygen would be of incomparably higher value than performing the same feat using oxygen. To scientific men it would be a demonstration of the capacity and adaptability of the human body. And the ordinary man would have his soul satisfied in a way that an oxygen climb never could satisfy it.

If the experiences of the 1922 expedition show anything, they show that Everest can be climbed with oxygen or it can be climbed without oxygen, but that it cannot be climbed by havering about between the one method and the other. A choice between them has to be made. The climber's mind must not be divided. He must approach Everest single-minded. His plan must be simple.

And two considerations should tell strongly against the oxygen. First, no really serviceable apparatus for supplying it has yet been devised. Second, and most important, the carrying up of the cylinders and apparatus necessitates the employment of a number of porters who would otherwise be available for carrying tents and supplies for the climbers. The number of porters to be had on the mountain is not unlimited. And if one method requires more porters than the other, the method which requires less should be preferred.

A party of enthusiastic scientists bent upon demonstrating

the use of oxygen might set out for Everest, plug away up its slopes cumbered with the unwieldy apparatus and eventually sit on the top inhaling oxygen. But if man wants to know what he can do by himself then he must go by himself. He may take a cylinder of oxygen for medicinal purposes as he would take a bottle of brandy. But he would not depend upon it. He would depend upon himself. And all our experience so far shows that he would have ample justification for the self-reliance.

Somervell at the end of this expedition said that he felt 'perfectly well at 27,000 feet.' Porters had carried loads to 25,000 feet and 25,500 feet. There was good hope, then, that they could be induced to carry at least one small tent to 27,000 feet. If that were possible a pair of climbers starting 'perfectly well' should be able to do the remaining 2000 feet without oxygen. And if that could be done, it would be an infinitely preferable, more satisfying and altogether more encouraging feat than an oxygen-aided ascent. It would show that the effects of altitude alone need not prevent men climbing any other mountain in the world.

Oxygenists might legitimately claim that if the expedition had concentrated upon oxygen – and upon oxygen alone – the summit might have been reached. It probably would have. But if it had we should have missed discovering the precious knowledge that men acclimatize themselves to the higher altitudes. We should have remained ignorant of the extent to which man by exercising his capacities can enlarge them. And we might have become increasingly dependent upon external stimulants instead of upon our own native energies for climbing high mountains. We might never have learned what it is in us to do. A branch of science might have won a success. But man would have lost a chance of knowing himself.

These, however, were lessons which we had not yet learned from the 1922 expedition and which it took a third expedition to teach us. We were still oscillating between faith in ourselves and faith in oxygen. We were relying too much on what physics and chemistry could do for us, and too little on what we could do for ourselves. So the next expedition was also supplied with oxygen.

But, as we shall see, it was a disastrous mistake. It complicated the plan of attack when it was above all things necessary that it should have been of the simplest possible description. And it entailed the employment of porters who might have been more effectively used in carrying tents and food.

This is, however, only being wise after the event. At the time it seemed foolish not to have oxygen, at least in reserve. And, even now, there are probably oxygen enthusiasts who would still recommend its use.

Chapter Seventeen

OTHER CONCLUSIONS

That there must be a second camp above the North Col – one at about 25,000 and another at about 27,000 feet – for a non-oxygen ascent to be successful, was the conclusion the expedition came to. Progress must be very slow on the mountain, however efficient the mountaineers, and however well acclimatized they may be. They had to take several breaths between each step. They might do much by economizing their efforts, preserving their balance, keeping their form, and moving rhythmically. Notwithstanding all this, they could not be expected to do more than 300 feet an hour on the last 2000 feet. A very early start at these great altitudes is almost an impossibility. And after reaching the summit they must allow time to get down if possible to the North Col. The pace coming down might be three times the pace going up. But four or five hours must be allowed. So a starting-off point for the summit must be fixed as near as possible to 27,000 feet. And what that means, anyone who has seen Nanga Parbat, 26,600 feet, from Kashmir, will realize. Yet it was a necessity to get porters to carry loads to even that prodigious height if the climbers were to gain the summit. That was the conclusion.

Another lesson learnt from the experience of this expedition was that the climbers must not be too old – must not be over forty and should be nearer thirty. If they are too old they do not readily acclimatize. And this was a valuable experience to have gained. For it had not been known before which were the better – the older or the younger. It might have been the case that the older, being more set and hardened, would stand the strain better. But however this might have been, they did not acclimatize, they did not rapidly adjust and adapt themselves to the new conditions of high altitudes, and were, consequently, less capable than the younger of climbing at very high heights.

On the other hand, if the climber were too young, though he might adapt himself more quickly to high-altitude conditions, he might give way under the strain. He might not have the stamina. Probably close round about thirty seemed to be the ideal age for an Everest climber.

And he must be of the tall, short-bodied, long-limbed type, that is, with not much weight to carry but with length of leg to lift it.

Good lung capacity is obviously necessary. Mallory and Finch were both of opinion that long, strong, deep breaths are necessary. Somervell, on the other hand, found rapid short breaths suited him best. It is too early to dogmatize. Each must carefully study himself and do what helps him most. But in either case good lungs and a strong heart are essentials.

As long as they could steadily plod along the climbers did very well, but any abnormal exertion put them out of their stride and distressed them much. Cooking their meals, putting on their boots, going out to fasten up the guy ropes – even getting into bed – upset them. All that could be done to reduce such exertions to the minimum was desirable.

A supporting party was another clear necessity. The first attempt suffered terribly through the want of one. Men making their supreme effort must be able to feel that behind them is some one ready to succour them if in distress, and anyhow to have a good warm meal ready for them on their return from the greatest day's work they are ever likely to put in again in their lives.

As to the obstacles and dangers an Everest expedition is likely to meet with, it was now well established that Everest was, in the language of the Alpine Club, 'an easy rock peak'. The outward-facing slabs of rock on the North Face – especially when sprinkled with snow – were dangerous and had to be treated with caution. But they did not constitute an insurmountable obstacle. And there was nothing in the remaining half mile not yet covered which would stand in the way of man reaching the summit.

The mountain itself was no obstacle. The weather was the hindrance – the terrific winds and the cold and the snow. The cold could be guarded against by the use of warm clothing; and Somervell gave a warning that the very process of acclimatization rendered the acclimatized the more open to frostbite. And against this future expeditions must take precautions.

Of the danger of snow the expedition had a terrible experience which will be a warning to all future expeditions. There is no need to enlarge upon it.

The wind is not such a danger as snow, but is a more constant hindrance. So frequent indeed were these raging winds that the climbers came to the conclusion that they must be taken as part of the normal state of things. When they are at their worst movement is out of the question. But considering the shortness of the time in which climbing operations are at all feasible climbers cannot afford to wait for a windless day. Unless there is a hurricane blowing they must climb, wind or no wind. But if this is to be done they must provide themselves and their porters with clothing as nearly wind-proof as it can be made; and provide tents equally impervious to the elements. Not that any material short of hardened steel could really withstand these Everest winds. But there are degrees of permeability in materials, and the least permeable which is also wearable and portable must be chosen.

These were valuable experiences to have gained, and if the next expedition could profit by them they would be much more likely to succeed.

Chapter Eighteen

THE THIRD EXPEDITION

A third expedition had now to be organized. For a third time permission had to be obtained from the Tibetan government, money found, a climbing party formed, stores and equipment collected in England, and a porter corps enlisted in India.

But now more time was available, for it was decided not to send out an expedition in the immediately following year but to wait till 1924. And a change in the chairmanship of the Mount Everest Committee occurred. It was the turn of the President of the Alpine Club to take the chair. And the President of the Alpine Club was General Bruce himself. He could combine in his own person, therefore, both the chairmanship of the committee and leadership of the expedition. It was a happy combination.

The question of a second-in-command who would lead on the mountain itself was not so easy to settle. Experience had shown that the men on the mountain must not be too old. Colonel Strutt, therefore, would not again be available. And a second-in-command who might on emergency have to take General Bruce's place must have knowledge of India and experience in dealing with Asiatics. Colonel Norton would be the very man if his services could be had. He was still young enough for climbing; and he could speak Hindustani and knew how to handle Indian hill men. Moreover, as the commander of a battery and as a Staff Officer, he had much experience in organization and leadership. But since the second Everest expedition he had been employed as Staff Officer in the Dardanelles and for some time it was questionable whether he would be available. However, the trouble there subsided; the military authorities in England proved amenable to persuasion; and Norton joined the expedition.

Mallory was a more delicate problem. It was in the highest degree desirable to have him. But was it fair to ask him? If he were invited he could not well refuse. Were the committee justified in virtually compelling him to go? He was a married man. He had already taken part in two expeditions. In the last he had been in two serious accidents, in one of which seven men had lost their lives. He had already played his part – and played it nobly. Could the committee, with any fairness, ask him to do more? On the other hand, might he not be deeply offended if he were *not* asked – he who had borne all the cold and burden of the day? Might he not be cruelly affronted if he were passed over? It was a difficult point to decide, and delicate feelers were sent out towards him to ascertain which way his wishes lay. The committee were satisfied that in his heart he wanted to go. An invitation was offered. And to the joy and relief of the committee he gladly accepted it.

Somervell, also, much to everyone's satisfaction, would be able to join the expedition. With his skill as a surgeon, his wide experience in the Great War, and his general popularity, he might have built himself up a big practice in England. And in

England he would have found fuller scope for exercising his talent in music and painting, and more congenial society in which to display it. But he had felt the call upon him to use his surgical skill in the service of the people of India and had joined a mission in Southern India. So he was near at hand and would be able to get away for four or five months to the Himalaya to take part in yet another attempt to reach the summit of Mount Everest.

Geoffrey Bruce was another old hand who would be available. So far, he had not had much training in the art and craft of mountaineering. Now he had been to Switzerland and acquired much that can be only learned among the expert climbers of the Alps.

Of the new men the most valuable addition was Mr N. E. Odell. He was a geologist and had not been able to leave his employment for the previous expedition – much as he had been wanted. Now, however, he was free for Everest. He was in Persia, but he could get away to India for a few months. He was of a splendid type, beautifully built, on almost perfect lines. He had great experience in Alpine mountaineering. And he was possessed of a calm, level disposition at the heart of which worked a firm determination. Much might be expected of a man like him; and he was not of the kind to belie expectations.

Of a different nature was Mr Bentley Beetham. He had not exactly the concentrated fire of Mallory, but he was perpetually boiling and bursting and bubbling over with keenness and enthusiasm – the kind of man that nothing less than a ton of bricks could keep down: nineteen hundredweight would have been of no use. And he too was an experienced mountaineer who had made great climbs in the Alps. By profession he was a schoolmaster. And it must be fortunate for the school that the Alps are fairly accessible, that he may annually let off much loose steam.

The third new climber was Hazard. He was an engineer by profession and had a great mountaineering record, and, having served in India as a sapper, knew something of Indian requirements.

Last of the climbers was Andrew Irvine. He was only twenty-two. He had not the training in the Alps which is so desirable. But Longstaff and Odell had seen him at work on the Oxford Spitzbergen expedition in 1923, and had strongly recommended that he should be included in the Everest expedition. He had twice rowed in the Oxford boat and was necessarily therefore of magnificent physique though perhaps of too heavy a build for an Everest climb, and in that respect not so perfect as Odell. His youth too might have been against him – but about that none could offer an authoritative opinion, for nothing was known as to the limits of age which were desirable. A man as young as he might acclimatize quicker. On the other hand, his system might be too young to stand the strain put on it.

But if he had not the mountaineering experience of the others, and if his youth might or might not be an advantage, what was certain was that in character and in mind he was admirably fitted. Of this he had already given proof. He was the kind of man who would readily fit into an expedition and keep it going, identify himself wholly with it, and naturally and habitually do the thing which would best help it along – not bothering about his own particular advantage but absorbed in the success of the venture. A quick-minded man, too, very much all there, and with a genius for mechanical contrivances. He was still an undergraduate at Oxford. But he promised so well and had so many proved capacities there was little hesitation in making the 'experiment'.

In India other important members of the expedition were to join. Someone with Indian experience was necessary for the purpose of managing the porters on the line of communication between the Base Camp and the mountain. Captain C. J. Morris had performed this duty on the previous expedition, but was not again available. His place was to be taken by Mr Shebbeare, of the Indian Forest Department. He knew these mountain people well and had the knack of handling them.

Finally, as medical officer and naturalist to the expedition, Major R. W. G. Hingston, of the Indian Medical Service, was chosen. He was not a mountaineer in the strict sense of the word, and his business would not be climbing. But he had travelled in the Pamirs – 'The Roof of the World' – and would be acquainted, therefore, with the conditions prevailing in Tibet, for there is much similarity between these two mountain regions. And, as an officer of the Indian Medical Service, he was accustomed to dealing with Asiatics. He was also known as a cheery companion and an ardent naturalist. He promised, therefore, to be a worthy successor of Wollaston and Longstaff.

Of these members was the third Everest expedition composed. But what about its finance? This was an anxious question, for, in one way and another, some £10,000 had to be raised to supplement what was already in hand. It was settled by the enterprise and spirit of Captain Noel. Noel, though not a climber, had been almost the keenest of all in seeing Everest climbed. And he now came forward with proposals for the cinematographic and photographic rights which enabled the expedition to be undertaken. He was financially supported by Mr Archibald Nettlefold and others. And to these two in particular it was due that the expedition could proceed.

Having obtained from the Tibetan government leave for a third expedition to proceed to Everest, having arranged the finance, and settled the composition of the party, the stores and equipment had to be bought, packed and dispatched. It might be thought that after the experience of two previous expeditions this would be a simple matter. But finality is never reached in organizing and equipping expeditions any more than in anything else. And Colonel Norton at the end of the expedition sat down with the members and together they suggested improvements which might still be made. The sum result of the experience of the three expeditions is worth recording, and perhaps here is as good a place as any for setting it down.

Norton was strongly of opinion that the leader of the expedition should have the last word in the selection of the party. He has to live and work with them and upon him the main responsibility rests. He, therefore, should have the final say in choosing the men.

Norton also considered that the main plan of campaign against the mountain should be settled in England before the expedition starts. This is an interesting point. One would have supposed that Tibet would be a better place than England for planning an attack on Everest. But Norton's point is that the scale of porters' equipment and the packing of the climbers' food for high camps largely depends upon the plan adopted. Another reason is that conditions on the Tibetan plateau in

April are not the most favourable for reconciling conflicting points of view. In other words, men's tempers are short at an altitude of 15,000 feet with the thermometer nearing zero and howling winds blowing. Members of the Tibet Mission of 1903 can also testify to that. A practical difficulty in the way of settling a plan in England is that important members may be at a distance; in the present case, for instance, Somervell was in Southern India, Odell was in Persia, and Geoffrey Bruce was in Northern India. But much can be done by correspondence and the general lines of attack could certainly be arranged.

Norton further advises that the Chairman of the Equipment Committee should be a prominent member of the party who has been on previous expeditions and should be responsible for supervising all departments, for keeping everybody up to time, and for having everything completely ready three or four months before shipment so that it can be properly inspected.

The tents seem to have been satisfactory – the Whymper tents and the Meade tents and the light Meade tents. And Norton himself invented a very useful and convenient mess tent for use in the march across Tibet and at the Base Camp.

'A moderately respectable coat or suit' should be taken by the leader of the expedition for wear when interviewing Tibetan officials, is another piece of advice. And when we remember that these officials are invariably arrayed in the most beautiful Chinese silks, and that most of them will probably never have seen a European before, we can see how necessary it is that at least the leader should present a respectable appearance on state occasions.

A well-stocked book box is also recommended. And most travellers would endorse Norton's opinion. Books serve to get the mind away from the discomforts and sordidness of exploration and to maintain the spirit. They are invaluable. Also books read on an exploration are remembered: the mind is then impressionable.

Geoffrey Bruce adds much useful advice about the equipment of the Indian personnel of an expedition. Major Hingston notes on the medical equipment, expressing approval of the Congo chest and the case of surgical instruments supplied, but suggesting certain changes and additions – suggesting also that equipment for high camps should be packed in separate boxes in England, and noting what the contents of each higher and higher camp-box should be. Somervell gives his views on climbing equipment at the high camps – on Meade tents, ice axes, ropes, crampons, rope ladders, sleeping bags, food, primus stoves, Meta fuel, thermos flasks, scientific instruments, and so on. Odell urges that a lighter oxygen apparatus should be employed. The total weight should be if possible 15 lb and at most 20 lb. If reserve cylinders are dumped upon the mountain a climber need not carry more than two cylinders. Shebbeare deals with the question of transport across Tibet. And Beetham gives recommendations about the running of the mess. Special cases for high camps should all be sent ready packed from London so as to save the necessity of making them up in Tibet. And boxes containing a complete supply of food for so many days should be made up in London for use on the march and numbered A1, A2, A3 – B1, B2, B3 – C1, C2, C3, etc., and the contents of all A cases should be alike but different from the contents of B; and B should be different from C; and C from D. They would be used in the order A1, B1, C1, D1; A2, B2, etc., for by this method constant repetition of the same food would be avoided – a repetition which causes lack of appetite. Sugar, milk, jam and tea, he said, disappeared most rapidly.

All these observations in great detail will be found in Section VI, 'The Organization of the Expedition', in *The Fight for Everest*, Colonel Norton's book on the 1924 expedition.

But by far the most important question in regard to equipment was the question of providing oxygen equipment. Should or should not oxygen be taken? Unfortunately the decision was made to take it – and in this decision the present writer shared. The lesson of acclimatization had not yet been thoroughly learned. Somervell was not in England to press his conclusions for trusting in acclimatization as persuasively as he had pressed for the use of oxygen in 1922. Its use had certainly enabled men to climb to 27,000 feet. It *might* be the only means of enabling them to reach 29,000 feet. It would be better to have it there as a stand-by anyhow – so the argument ran – and so quantities of oxygen cylinders and the usual cumbersome apparatus were provided for the expedition.

Chapter Nineteen

DARJILING TO RONGBUK

Bruce and Norton started out to India ahead of the bulk of the party and reached Delhi on February 18th, 1924. There the late Lord Rawlinson, Commander-in-Chief in India, gave them every assistance and encouragement. The son of an old president of the Royal Geographical Society, he was keenly interested in the expedition, and he made the way easy for Captain Geoffrey Bruce to join the expedition and for the services of four Gurkha non-commissioned officers to be placed at General Bruce's disposal.

On March 1st the nucleus of the expedition was formed at Darjiling – General Bruce, Norton, Geoffrey Bruce and Shebbeare of the Indian Forest Department. Shebbeare was new. 'He was a glutton for work and with him discomforts count not,' says Bruce. He was to act as Transport Officer, and with his aid preparations went on apace. Nothing deterred by the death of seven porters on the previous expedition, numbers of hill men, Sherpas, Bhotias and others, were rolling up anxious to be taken on. Several were coming for the third time. About three hundred presented themselves and seventy were engaged. Karma Paul was again taken on as interpreter, together with his assistant Gyaljen. And one of those shy, gentle Lepchas, inhabitants of Sikkim, who make such wonderful collectors, was engaged for service under the naturalist, Hingston.

Soon the rest of the expedition began to come in – Somervell from Travancore, Odell from Persia, Hingston from Baghdad, and finally Mallory, Irvine, Beetham and Hazard from England. All were assembled under the cheery leadership of General Bruce, again thoroughly in his element with his hill men round him and the great Himalayan peaks ahead; while Noel was making arrangements for an elaborate cinematograph record of the expedition.

On March 25th, they left Darjiling with the intention of reaching the Base Camp under Mount Everest well by May 1st, so as to have the whole of May and as much of June as the monsoon would spare them for the march up the East Rongbuk Glacier and assault upon the mountain.

As a rule, marching through Sikkim one has very few chances of seeing the wonderful mountain that dominates the whole country. Kangchenjunga is usually hidden by the nearer ranges, or, when a ridge is reached from which it should be seen, is hidden in mists. But on this occasion Bruce had a rare view of it. From the minor Kapup Pass he saw the whole Kangchenjunga massif. And it was not staring blatantly at him in cold sharp outline; it was suffused in that mysterious haze so characteristic of this region – a deep bluey violet haze which gives to even solid mountains a spiritual effect. The lower slopes were swallowed up in blueness, while all above the snow line seemed, says Bruce, to be detached from any earthly base and to be floating in mid-air.

It is visions like this which make up to a mountaineer for the sordid discomforts and hardships of travel. And a man who has been in among the mountains and wrestled strongly with them appreciates them in this ethereal aspect more than those who have only viewed them from a distance ever can.

In due course, the expedition arrived at Phari, and here on the edge of the Tibetan plateau made their preparations for the march across it. All the tents were pitched and inspected. Stores were assorted. Members of the expedition were submitted to physiological tests by the enthusiastic Hingston. And Bruce engaged in a mighty battle with the Dzongpen over rates of payment. Like most Tibetan officials the Dzongpen was well-mannered. But he was feeble, grasping and avaricious; and he was really in the hands of his subordinates, who were, in Bruce's words, a truculent crowd of cheerful rascals, who, quite clearly, had not taken on their duties for health's sake alone.

But Phari is in telegraphic communication with Lhasa. And communication with Lhasa now spelt good, not ill. Knowing that a telegram had reached the Dzongpen from Lhasa ordering him to give the expedition every assistance, Bruce wrote out a telegram to Lhasa complaining of his treatment; and, using this as a weapon, was able to get an agreement drawn up and signed in full Durbar.

The expedition then left Phari full of spirits, but soon to meet with grave misfortune. Bruce, according to the physiological test which had been applied at Phari, was in better condition than when he left London. But crossing the Pass into Tibet proper, the expedition experienced that bitter wind which blows across it, and the next morning Bruce was down with a severe go of malaria – so severe that he had to be taken back to Sikkim forthwith and to hand over the conduct of the expedition to Norton.

It was a bitter blow to Bruce, for his whole heart for years had been set on climbing Everest, and if he could not at his age be among the actual climbers he could be there at the base organizing the assault and encouraging the assailants. Now he would have to turn his back upon them just when he might be most useful. It was hard, indeed, for him. And it was a serious matter for the expedition. The organization could be done, and was done, just as well by others. But what no one could ever do as well as Bruce was the encouragement. Bruce is a kind of benevolent volcano in perpetual eruption of good cheer. And of such irrepressible fun that no amount of misfortune can ever quell him. This quality was valuable enough with the Englishmen: it was of ten times greater value with the natives. From the Base Camp he would have been emitting volumes of cheerfulness which would have affected the whole expedition. And, in the event, it was found that this was just exactly what was so sorely needed.

Norton, therefore, now took up the reins from Bruce. And in one respect this was an advantage. For Norton had been actually on the mountain before, and he would be one of the climbers again. And this was an advantage which Bruce could not have. Norton had not the same knowledge of the natives, or of the Himalaya, that Bruce had. But he was still young enough to be of the climbers.

And Norton had, like Bruce, that quality which is of such inestimable value in all members of an expedition but which is specially necessary in a leader. It is the same quality that expresses itself in such phrases as 'country first', 'ship before self', and which in the present case might be rendered as 'summit first'. Norton might have argued on the same lines as a great polar explorer – not an Englishman – reasoned with himself: he might have said, 'The main burden and responsibility of the expedition is on me. To me therefore is due the honour, and I am entitled to ask the others to sacrifice themselves in order that I should have the better chance of reaching the summit.' There is something fair and reasonable in such argument. The leader of an expedition does have the responsibility. He receives the blame in case of failure and should have the praise in case of success. But Norton took the view that the attainment of the summit was the main consideration and that who attained it and had the honour was of secondary account. He was prepared to be a member of the climbing party. But whether he was fit to partake in the final effort he would leave to the impartial judgement of the two most competent climbers, namely, Mallory and Somervell.

This public-spirited action gave great encouragement to the expedition. If he had taken the opposite course, and asked the members to sacrifice themselves for him, doubtless they would have done it. But they would hardly have done it with the same enthusiasm as they did when the matter was left to their own choice. And how Mallory, the man chiefly concerned, for he had been in all three expeditions and had originally discovered the way up, viewed the matter, is fortunately on record. In a letter dated April 19th, 1924, to a member of the Mount Everest Committee, he wrote:

'I must tell you, what Norton can't say in a dispatch, that we have a splendid leader in him. He knows the whole "bandobast" from A to Z, and his eyes are everywhere, is personally acceptable to everyone and makes us all feel happy, is always full of interest, easy and yet dignified, or rather never losing dignity, and a tremendous adventurer – he's dead keen to have a dash with the non-oxygen party; he tells me (and I tell you confidentially, as I'm sure he wouldn't have it broadcasted) that when the time comes he must leave it to me in consultation with Somervell to decide whether he'll be the right man for the job. Isn't that the right spirit to bring to Mount Everest?'

This testimony from Mallory is specially valuable because Mallory might well have resented Norton having the leadership. Mallory had the higher reputation as a mountaineer and had been connected with these expeditions from their inception. He would have been only human if he had thought that he and not Norton should now be leader. And we must note this also about Norton's self-effacing action – that it was taken when the members of the expedition thought that they were certain to reach the top this time; and Mallory himself in this same letter says that he could not believe that more than one attempt would be necessary. He believed that Everest would fall at the first assault. To the members of the first party would therefore fall the honour; and naturally every one would wish to be of that party.

The plans for the attack they now began seriously to discuss. They were delayed four days at Khamba Dzong waiting for transport, and they made use of the delay to go exhaustively into the whole question. It would seem to be a fairly simple operation; but it was complicated by two factors, apart from the uncertainty of the weather. The first factor was the necessity for making arrangements for oxygen-using climbers as well as

for non-oxygen. The second consideration was that, in those
parts of the assault where porters were employed, a
Hindustani- or Nepalese-speaking climber had to form one of
the party.

As far back as Christmas, Norton had drawn up a plan and
circulated it among the members for discussion. Mallory had
disagreed with certain aspects; and at Darjiling and Phari
discussions had taken place between Norton, Mallory, Somervell and Geoffrey Bruce. But even now at Khamba Dzong
agreement had not been reached. It was not till they arrived at
Tinki Dzong, on April 17th, that a plan was evolved which met
with the approval of all. It is described by Mallory with whom
it originated.

(*a*) A and B with about fifteen porters start from Camp IV on
the North Col, establish Camp V at about 25,500 feet, and
descend.

(*b*) C and D, non-oxygen climbers, go to Camp V with
another fifteen porters, of whom seven carry loads. These
seven, having deposited their loads, descend while the other
eight sleep at Camp V.

(*c*) C and D, taking with them these eight porters, proceed
on the next day to establish Camp VII at 27,300 feet.

(*d*) E and F, with oxygen, on the same day as (*c*) start with
about ten porters from Camp IV, go without loads to Camp V;
from that point E and F take on the stores and oxygen
previously dumped at Camp V, and carry them about 1000 feet
higher and form Camp VI, at 26,500 feet.

(*e*) Then the two parties start next morning and hope to
meet on the summit.

The chief merits of this plan, in Mallory's opinion, were that the two parties could mutually support one another; that the camps could be established without waste of reserve climbers, for A and B would not have overexerted themselves; and that Camp VI could be established without a collapse of the porters. Even if the first attempt failed there would still be perhaps four climbers available for a second effort, and the camps would be there ready for them.

This was the simplest plan that could be evolved after prolonged discussion. And even then it would not be possible to put in just any climber as A, B, C, D, E, F. Regard must be had as to who could speak Nepalese and who could safely use oxygen. But, if no simpler plan than this could be thought of, one disadvantage of using oxygen was plainly visible: it necessarily complicated a plan.

Poor Mallory himself suffered through the necessity of fitting men into the different pairs and allotting the tasks so as best to ensure success for the whole enterprise. The non-oxygen party he considered would have the better adventure. It had always been his pet plan to climb the mountain with a non-oxygen party, making two camps above the North Col. And he was disappointed that the parties had now to be arranged so that he was to be with the oxygen party. It had been decided that one party should be led by Somervell and one by him. And he was chosen for the oxygen party because it was assumed it would be less exhausted than the other and in a position to help the other and be responsible for the descent; while Somervell was chosen for the non-oxygen party because, on his last year's performance, it seemed that he would be more likely to recover and be useful again later. It was a disappointment to Mallory that matters should have so arranged themselves. He consoled himself with the thought that the conquest of the mountain was the main consideration and his own feelings secondary. His part, in any case, would be sufficiently interesting and might, he thought, give him the best chance of all of reaching the top.

Either Norton or Hazard, according as which proved the fitter of the two at the time, would go with Somervell; and Irvine would go with Mallory, because Irvine had displayed such ingenuity and industry in remedying the defects of the oxygen apparatus. Odell and Geoffrey Bruce would have the important task of fixing Camp V. Beetham would probably not be available. He was suffering from dysentery and was so bad that it had almost been decided to send him back.

It having been settled that Mallory should be one of the oxygen-users he threw himself into the oxygen plans with all the enthusiasm that he might have had if he had been an advocate for its use from the first. He loaded himself with the apparatus and climbed hills and convinced himself that it was a 'perfectly manageable load'. And he determined to carry as few cylinders as possible, but to go fast and rush the summit.

His companion also having been fixed he made a point of establishing a strong partnership with Irvine so that the two might work efficiently and willingly together. They talked together and went out together and got to know each other well so that they might instinctively act together when the strain came.

And the whole expedition were remarkably hopeful as they marched across Tibet making their plans. They felt confident of success. They were well up to time. The weather was fine, and warmer than in 1922. And they felt themselves to be a fit and united party of climbers – 'a really strong lot', as Mallory expressed it, and 'a much more even crowd than in '22'.

The porter corps, seventy strong, also was good. They were all of Mongolian stock, that is either Bhotias or Sherpas – the Bhotias being of Tibetan stock living in the Darjiling district or Sikkim; and the Sherpas being of Tibetan stock but living in the higher valleys of Nepal. They had been carefully picked according as they approximated to a certain type which experience had shown was the best adapted for climbing the mountain. That is, they were light and wiry rather than heavy and muscular. And they were intelligent men of a good class so as to stand the stress of high-altitude conditions. To deal with, both individually and en masse, they were, says Norton, singularly like a childish edition of the British soldier, many of whose virtues they shared. They had the same high spirit for a tough or dangerous job; the same ready response to quip and jest. And, as with the British soldier, the rough character who is a perpetual nuisance when drink and the attractions of civilization tempt him astray often came out strongest when 'up against it' in circumstances where the milder man failed.

Throughout the journey across Tibet they were never burdened with heavy loads. They were reserved for the big task on the mountain itself and kept in the best possible condition by being lightly exercised and supplied with good food, clothing and tents. Not that carrying loads is any very serious matter for them, as they are accustomed from their childhood to fetch and carry water and grain for the upkeep of their homes.

Absorbed in their plans, thoroughly pleased with themselves and their prospects, and only regretting the absence of their cheery chief, the expedition made its way across Tibet by the now well-known route. The early mornings were usually still and gloriously sunny and they would breakfast in the open at about seven o'clock while the big tent was being packed and dispatched on ahead on a pair of fast mules. By 7.30 or 8, the whole expedition would be stringing out on the march. The climbers would ride about half the way, for the experience of 1922 had shown the necessity of saving their energies for the work ahead. About 11.30 they would sit down by twos and threes in some spot sheltered from the wind which invariably arises about then, and eat a light lunch of biscuit and cheese, chocolate and raisins.

By two o'clock, though occasionally as late as seven, they would usually reach their new camp. There the mess tent would already be pitched and a more substantial lunch and tea would be ready. Soon the tents and baggage would begin to arrive. Dinner would be served at about 7.30. And by 8.30 they would go to bed, the thermometer at night generally falling to about 10 degrees.

Skekar Dzong was reached on April 23rd. The Dzongpen rode out to meet the expedition, greeted them most court- eously and promised every assistance in his power. And he kept his word: fresh transport was ready in two days. And he proved himself a straightforward and efficient gentleman with whom Norton found it a pleasure to deal, and entirely master in his own house. Through some slip a mistake had been made in calculating the cost of the transport – and the mistake was in favour of the British. But when Norton pointed it out to him the Dzongpen refused to go back on an undertaking he had once given. Some of the most handsome and costly presents were bestowed upon this generous official, but Norton subsequently heard that what he really hankered after was a cheap camp chair and a pair of snow goggles. The latter could be given, but no chair could be spared at the time and Norton accordingly sent it later from Darjiling.

On April 26th the expedition crossed the Pang La, nearly 18,000 feet, and from a small hill above it Norton had a glorious view of the great Himalayan Range. Just opposite, and only thirty-five miles distant, was Mount Everest itself. On the left of it were Makalu and Kangchenjunga, and on the right were Gyachung Kang, Cho Uyo and Gosainthan. So he had before him the highest mountain in the world and several of those which most nearly approached it; and he must have seen nearly 200 miles of the range. And that nothing might be lacking from the grandeur of the view, he observes, each of the giants is so spaced from its neighbours that none is dwarfed, and each stands dominating the serried ranks of lesser peaks stretching in a jagged line from horizon to horizon. On these mountains all is snow and ice above 20,000 feet except where the cliffs are too sheer for snow to lie. But there is one exception: by some freak of the inclination of the rock to the impact of the perpetual north-west wind the northern face of the whole pyramid of Mount Everest for 6000 feet is at this season almost bare of snow.

In imagination the climbers climbed Everest by every conceivable route. They made a certainty of it. Then they turned to Makalu to climb that too. But there they were defeated. Not even in imagination could they climb it. Many a long year must pass before Makalu is recognized among the accessible peaks of the Himalaya.

On April 28th they passed through the ugly desolate

country where the mountains resemble brown lumps, and the valley bottom is bounded by lines of moraines like railway embankments, which form the approach to the Everest region, and encamped just in front of the Rongbuk Monastery. The next day they reached the site of the old Base Camp four miles further up.

They were up to time – two days indeed before it. And so methodically had every arrangement been made that they were able to get to work at once with the minimum of delay. Nearly three hundred yak-loads of provision boxes, rolls of bedding and stores of all sorts dumped higgledy-piggledy off the yaks were soon sorted into orderly lines and piles. And a steadily increasing dump of boxes and bundles, each appropriately labelled, represented the loads which would be started off the very next day for Camp I on the East Rongbuk Glacier on the shoulders of the local Tibetan porters who had been specially enlisted for the purpose through the good offices of the Shekar Dzongpen.

Chapter Twenty

UP THE GLACIER

So far so good – but no further. All that man by forethought
and pre-arrangement could do had been done. The elements
were now to have *their* say. No sooner had the expedition
arrived at the Base Camp than down came the snow, blotting
out the landscape, whirling about the men and making them
bitterly cold. It was the preliminary round in the struggle. And
the party faced their enemy muffled to their eyes in full outfit
of woollen and windproof clothes, ear-flapped caps and long
mits, and worked without stopping till dusk, by which time
they were ready to send off a hundred and fifty porters on the
following day – April 30th.

Norton's intention was to make the first attempt on the
mountain on May 17th. But much previous arrangement was
still necessary. Camps I, II and III on the glacier had to be
established and stocked; the route to the North Col had to be
reconnoitred by a party of expert climbers, as it would surely
have changed since 1922, and might be even more dangerous
than it proved then; Camp IV must then be established and
stocked with stores and oxygen both for itself and the higher
camps; then Camp V at about 25,500 feet had to be similarly

established and stocked; and finally Camp VI at about 26,500 feet, and Camp VII at about 27,200 feet. All this had to be done before the actual attempt could be made.

And all through the workers would have to be contending against high altitude *malaise*. Besides the cold and the wind and the snow they would have to be fighting that peculiar depression which comes on at about 16,000 feet and makes work a burden. The Base Camp was situated at about 16,800 feet and here it began. The least exertion, such as getting into a sleeping bag or putting on boots, was exhausting. Even lighting a pipe was a business, for the smoker's breath would give out about the same moment as the match, and the pipe would go out before breath was recovered. And every stage beyond the Base Camp was a stage higher and the depression and exhaustion would become progressively worse. Norton confesses that the first trip to Camp I was pain and grief to him. Merely from the weight of his ice axe his right arm and shoulder became so weary that he thought he would have to find a lighter implement. Walking was a labour and in the keenest air there was no exhilaration: rather was there an indefinable feeling of discomfort and distress.

To such distress men became to a certain extent 'acclimatized'. Even so, there is no spring in their activities. They are not the men they are below the 16,000-feet level. And it was in these depressing conditions that the hard preparatory work had to be done.

The hardest of this work would naturally fall on the porters; and to save them as far as possible the hundred and fifty Tibetans whom Norton had enlisted, were used for establishing the first two camps on the glacier. The arrangement with them was that they should be paid at the rate of a shilling a day and given some rations. They were not to be employed on snow or ice, and were to be quickly released when their work was done so that they might return to sow their fields. Tents they did not expect and they were quite prepared to sleep out in the open, even at 18,000 feet.

Further, to save the climbers as far as possible, the Gurkha non-commissioned officers were employed to establish Camps I and II.

On April 30th the work of forming the camps began. The Tibetans consisted of men, women and boys. The average load would be about 40 lb. And Geoffrey Bruce, who was in charge of the operations, tried to hand out the lightest loads to the women and boys. His efforts were useless. They were contrary to the custom of the country. The Tibetan method of distributing loads was simpler and to Tibetans more satisfactory. They all wear round the tops of their boots prettily-woven garters of distinct colouring and each can immediately recognize his or her own colours. And in distributing loads the distributor collects a garter from each carrier, shuffles the lot, and then throws one on each load. The owner of each garter then claims his or her load and goes off without complaint. This was the method Geoffrey Bruce now used and the Tibetans went off singing and joking, as is their way.

Two of the three Gurkha NCOs conducting the convoy had been with the 1922 expedition and could be relied on to reconnoitre the route from Camp I to Camp II without assistance from the climbers. They had also the responsible task of taking charge of a glacier camp each, seeing to the feeding and welfare of every one in it, and supervising the arrivals and departures of convoys.

Camp I was – for the Rongbuk Glacier – a snug retreat. It was situated on the East Rongbuk stream, a few hundred yards above its junction with the main Rongbuk Glacier; and it caught all the sunshine and missed most of the wind. The 'sangars' built by the previous expedition were still in good condition, and by stretching the flies of the Whymper tents over them, comfortable shelters were made.

From Camp I seventy-five Tibetans were sent back to the Base Camp and seventy-five retained for the establishment of Camp II. On the two following days they did this and returned full of cheer. The performances of the women were especially remarkable. One carried her child of about two years old on the top of her 40-lb load from 17,500 feet to 19,800 feet, deposited her load there, carried the child back again, and expressed her readiness to repeat the journey if necessary. Of the seventy-five who had returned to the Base Camp, fifty-two, however, disappeared without any special reason and so laid an additional burden on the remainder. In spite of this, by May 2nd, all loads had been deposited in Camp II, and on the same evening the Tibetans, having arrived at the Base Camp, were given a big feed and a little extra pay. They went off next day displaying great satisfaction with their lot.

For the future the expedition would have to depend on themselves. Their next task was the transportation from Camp II of all the stores for Camp III and the mountain camps. And for this work the Nepalese porter corps would have to be brought into action. It was divided into two parties of twenty each, and twelve were kept in reserve. The first party was to carry stores and equipment to Camp III and remain based there ready to carry on a camp to the North Col. The second party, leaving the Base Camp a day later, was to move to Camp II and work between that and Camp III. The reserve party was to remain in the Base Camp ready to replace casualties.

The first party set out on May 3rd. It was led by Mallory and consisted of two pairs of climbers besides the porters. Mallory and Irvine were to help with the establishment of Camp III and remain there for a few days to acclimatize and to test their oxygen apparatus. Odell and Hazard were to push on from Camp III, reconnoitre, and construct the route up the North Col.

It was a cold, stormy day with threatening clouds when the first party of climbers and porters left the Base Camp, and half the porters lagged badly: they had added a good deal on their own account in the way of blankets, etc., to their already heavy loads. In consequence, Mallory left behind five loads not urgently required, and utilized the five porters for carrying these blankets on the next day.

Camp II was reached on May 4th. It looked most uninviting. No tents had been provided here for the porters, as the intention had been to build comfortable huts or 'sangars', using the flies of the Whymper tents for roofs, and this work had now to be done. Mallory and Irvine with three or four men started work; others joined in when they had rested; and an oblong sangar about seven feet in breadth was constructed. Then Mallory and Odell reconnoitred a way up the glacier towards what would be Camp III. They climbed a hump from which the whole glacier could be seen rising to the south, and they eventually found a simple way along a stony trough through the high fantastic ice pinnacles into which the glacier is melted in this part.

The night of May 4th–5th was appalling – very cold with a violent wind and a considerable snow fall. The men were long in turning out of their tents and cooking their food. There was further difficulty about loads – about what rations, blankets and cooking pots could be left behind. And lastly the question who was and who was not fit to go on had to be settled. A start could not be made till 11 a.m.

And then the way up the glacier which had been so well marked the evening before had now been obliterated with snow. The glacier which had before looked innocent enough was far from innocent now. The wind had blown the higher surfaces clear, and these surfaces were hard, smooth, rounded ice, almost as hard as glass with never a trace of roughness, while between the projecting lumps lay the new powdery snow. Much labour had, in consequence, to be expended in cutting steps in the ice or making steps in the snow. The trough itself, which was about fifty feet deep and extended a third of the way up, formed fairly good going. But when they came out on to the open glacier the wind was blowing maliciously, and, as they rounded the corner of the North Peak, it blew straight at them from off the icy North Col.

The porters were now nearly exhausted. They were feeling the altitude badly, and progress was a bitter experience. Camp III was not reached till 6.30. It was cold even then. It was too late to make a comfortable camp; and climbers and porters suffered greatly during the night.

Mallory recognized at once that the high altitude sleeping sacks intended for Camp IV and upwards must be used here also – so much severer was the cold than they had experienced before. But these bags were still at Camp II. He therefore determined to return next morning to that Camp and bring them up.

The sun strikes the tents early at Camp III and Mallory was able to get off about seven, after leaving directions that half the porters should be sent a quarter of the way down to Camp II in order to meet the porters coming up and help them in with the most important loads. He was delayed by making a fruitless effort to find a better way on to the glacier, and unfortunately did not meet the second party till after they had left Camp II. It was too late to turn them back so he led them on towards Camp III. According to the original plan, they should have carried their loads to that Camp and then returned to Camp II. This was not, however, now possible, for they had overloaded themselves with extra blankets intending to sleep there – an intention which Mallory had to frustrate as things in Camp III were bad enough already. He therefore made them dump their loads as near as they could reach to Camp III while retaining enough energy to carry them back to Camp II, and from this dump he sent them back, while going on himself to Camp III. His own first party was demoralized enough by the cold and altitude: he did not want the second party knocked up too.

Arrived back in Camp III he found little had been done in his absence. The three climbers were all new men and not yet acclimatized. They as well as the porters were feeling the cold and altitude. And not one of the porters was considered fit to carry a load. Not one had therefore been sent to meet the ascending party; and very little of even wall-building had been done. But Odell and Irvine went down to the dump and fetched a few special necessities such as Primus stoves.

On the night of May 6th–7th, the thermometer fell to 21½

degrees below zero, that is 53½ degrees of frost. It was the greatest cold that had been experienced on these expeditions, and coming on men who were depressed and weakened by an altitude of 21,000 feet it was acutely felt. Mallory himself had kept warm in the night, but even he was not well in the morning. Odell and Irvine were distinctly unfit. No porters were fit to carry loads and several were too unwell to be kept at Camp III at all: they had to be almost pulled from their tents. One of them had hardly a spark of life in him; his feet were so swollen that his boots had to be pulled on without socks; he was almost incapable of walking and had to be supported. Eventually the sick were made up in three parties; each party was roped; and these were dispatched downward in charge of the NCO. They staggered wearily down the glacier and arrived at Camp II almost in a state of collapse.

Meanwhile, Hazard, who was suffering less than his companions, had been sent down to the dump with a few of the fittest to meet a few of the fittest of the second party who would be coming up from Camp II. The meeting was effected and seven more loads were got to Camp III. But that was all. Nothing had been done to establish the camp in a more comfortable manner. And the *morale* of the first party had, in Mallory's words, 'gone to blazes'.

This was the situation which confronted Norton when he arrived at Camp II on May 7th; and he immediately set to to retrieve it. All the stores and tents intended for the higher camps were ruthlessly broken open and distributed to the suffering porters, high-altitude tents were pitched, high-altitude sleeping bags were issued, priceless stores of Meta solidified spirits were broached; the capacity of Camp II was doubled for the night, and some degree of comfort was afforded. And on May 8th, when Mallory arrived again from Camp III, and Geoffrey Bruce from the Base Camp, definite plans for the future were worked out. He wisely decided to rest the sick from the first party at Camp II, while Somervell, who had arrived with Norton and who was a great favourite with the men, having a happy way of getting the best out of them, should take the second party as far as the dump without loads and get them to carry from there to Camp III sufficient stores and bedding to make the camp habitable. If the remains of the first party could be pulled together they were to be utilized in keeping Camp III supplied from Camp II. Shebbeare, whose knowledge of the men and their language was of such value, was to be called up from the Base Camp to Camp II. And Hazard was to relieve Shebbeare at the base and look after the money and the fuel and meat arrangement. Thus did Norton courageously strive to stem the tide of misfortune which had set in.

Geoffrey Bruce had also brought with him the reserve porters. Being fresh they could do most of the heavy carrying, and their energy and keenness put new heart into the others. So, on May 9th, Norton, Mallory, Somervell, and Geoffrey Bruce, with twenty-six porters, were able to start for Camp III, carrying stores, some for the dump and some to go through to Camp III.

It seemed as if now the situation really had been retrieved. The contrary was the case. The elements had worse still in store. Snow began to fall soon after the party left camp and the fall increased as the day wore on. Wind also increased. And by the time Camp III was reached the wind and snow had attained the dimensions of a blizzard. The camp was a picture of desolation. Though situated in the only possible place for a camp it caught every icy blast that blew. No one was moving about it, and it seemed utterly lifeless. The terrible blizzard, coming immediately on the top of their previous hardships, had knocked all the spirits and energy out of the remaining porters. They stayed huddled up in their tents and many of them were so apathetic they would not attempt to cook for themselves, even when stoves and oil were pushed inside their tents. Fortunately, the eight stalwarts from the reserve (whom Geoffrey Bruce had brought on after sending back from the dump the remainder of the twenty-six) were able to help cook and generally to comfort the others. But nothing else could be done, for the fierceness of the wind made movement outside a tent almost impossible, and after a hasty meal every one turned in to his sleeping bag, where at any rate warmth could be found.

Outside, the blizzard continued with unabated violence through the night, and the light powdery snow was driven into the tents covering everything to a depth of an inch or two. The discomfort was acute. At the slightest movement of the body a miniature avalanche of snow would drop inside the sleeping bag and melt there into a cold wet patch.

Next day – May 10th – the snow ceased but the wind increased and drove before it the freshly fallen powdery snow in incessant gusts. It was now apparent that more climbers than were necessary should not be kept at Camp III: they only consumed stores and fuel and became worn out. And as Mallory and Irvine had borne the brunt of the hardship so far they were sent down to Camp II where they had a more peaceful time with Beetham and Noel.

The wind was still tearing across the glacier, snatching up the snow and hurling it through the camp. But, nothing daunted, Norton and Somervell with seventeen porters, found their way down to the dump about a mile from the camp and brought up nineteen loads, each Englishman carrying a load himself. When the porters returned they were completely played out. Struggling against the piercing wind had rid them of all their strength: they simply flopped into their tents and lay there. It was fortunate for them that while they were away Bruce and Odell had prepared a hot meal for everyone. They now forced the porters to eat and drink, took off their boots and saw them safely tucked into their sleeping bags.

As evening came on the wind blew still harder in tremendous gusts from every direction. It appeared to be shot in the air over the North Col, the Rápiu La, and the Hlakpa La, and then from some point high in the zenith it would descend on the little tents and shake them as a terrier would worry rats in a rat pit. That night the tents were again filled with snow. The noise of the wind and the wild flapping of the tents made sleep impossible. And the thermometer fell to 7 degrees below zero.

At dawn on the 11th the tempest was still raging; and at 9 a.m. the temperature was still below zero. The North Col would evidently not be practicable for several days. The much-enduring second party of porters had now been reduced to very much the same forlorn condition as the first. There was nothing for it but a retreat before the elements – and a retreat right back to the Base Camp where the whole expedition could have a chance of recuperating.

Yet even retreat was a struggle. The men were huddled in their tents, not caring whether they lived or died. Even the idea of withdrawing to the Base Camp with its comforts, warmth and good food, left them unmoved. They had almost to be dug out. But Geoffrey Bruce rose to the occasion. Taking up a commanding position in the centre of the camp he issued his orders in the very teeth of the gale – stinging words for the merely inert, much sympathy for the really sick, lesser sympathy for those who thought they were worse than they actually were. Gradually the tents were struck and packed in bags and boxes; bedding, stores, and fuel were all neatly dumped; such loads as were to be taken down the glacier were fairly apportioned; and eventually a comparatively cheerful party turned their backs on what an hour before had been Camp III, and which was now something resembling a neat pile of stones. May 11th was Geoffrey Bruce's day.

Instructions had been sent on for the withdrawal to the base. By the evening of the 11th, Mallory, Beetham, Irvine and Noel were at the Base Camp; Somervell and Odell with half the porters were at Camp I; and Norton and Geoffrey Bruce were at Camp II. Next day these two latter continued their way to the base, leaving tents and stores as they stood at Camp II ready for reoccupation. Somervell at Camp I had his hands full, for casualties were mounting up, and there were some very sick men. The worst case was Shamsher, one of the Gurkha NCOs, who was practically insensible owing to a clot of blood on the brain. Manbahadur, the cobbler, was also in a fearful condition with both his feet frostbitten up to the ankles. Another man was down with severe pneumonia. And many had minor ailments. All were got away except Shamsher, who could not be moved; so an NCO and two porters were left to look after him.

By the afternoon of the 12th all except these were assembled at the Base Camp. Bleak as it had seemed on their first arrival a fortnight before, it was now a real haven of rest, with warm spacious tents, hot food in plenty, and luxurious camp beds. Best of all, Hingston had arrived the day before and was there in the nick of time to cheer up the party and administer comfort to the sick and needy.

So ended round one with the mountain.

Chapter Twenty-One

DISASTER RETRIEVED

At this time more than any other General Bruce was missed. His bursting good cheer, his immoderate laughter over the tiniest jests, his capacity for light-heartedly brushing all difficulty aside, would have been worth a whole new porter corps at this juncture. And even to Norton himself Bruce, fresh here at the base, unwearied by a forty-eight-hour fight with a blizzard at 21,000 feet, would have been a welcome revivant. Norton was hardened to the roughs of life, for he had been in the retreat from Mons and through the Great War. But tempers are known to get frayed above 15,000 feet; you can be very stoical, and quite even-tempered, at sea level, and very cross and despondent at 21,000 feet. To him it must have been maddening to see the results of half a year's careful planning and organization caught up in the gust of a blizzard and tossed to the skies. And he might easily have lost control of his temper and lowered still further the depression of members. These other members of the expedition might also have lost theirs and got into a carping, 'grousing' mood. A rot might easily have set in and the spring gone out of the expedition if the leader had not kept himself tightly together. Such things have happened much nearer the sea level than even the Base Camp. It is to the credit of Norton and the other members that nothing of the sort did occur, and that they immediately buckled to, making a new plan to replace the one so rudely shattered to pieces.

The first necessity was to restore the spirit of the porters. They had so far had the worst experience and they must be properly cheered. And the most effective mode of encouragement proved to be the blessing of the lama at Rongbuk. This was what the men themselves most wanted. Many of them were Hindus and the lama was Buddhist. That did not matter. What they wanted was the blessing of a man of God. They might not have been particularly religious in ordinary times. But now they felt the near presence of the spirit of God. They were in close contact with death. Hardships and dangers they knew must be before them; more of this piercing cold and terrible wind; more of this ghastly depression; and dangers from avalanches and from a slip on the ice or the rock. At the risk of their lives they would be battling against all that the elements and a dangerous mountain could do against them and they wanted to be confident that what they were doing was worth the risk. If they had been a band of brigands setting out on some murderous raid they would not have dared to seek the blessing of a man of God. Being engaged on a noble enterprise they wanted to be reassured that God was with them in their work. The blessing of the holy lama would be for them this assurance. His life was spent in the pursuit and encouragement of goodness. He could speak to them for God. And if he gave them his blessing they could feel that God was with them and they would face the dangers and hardships of the future with a cheerful heart. This was their simple faith.

The very next day after the return to Base Camp Karma Paul, the interpreter, was sent to the Rongbuk Monastery to ask the lama to bless the men. The lama agreed, and on the appointed day – May 15th – the whole expedition, climbers, Gurkhas, and porters, proceeded four miles down the valley to be blessed, each man being given two rupees to offer to the lama. On arrival the men were told to remain in the larger outer court while the climbers were taken up to the lama's antechamber where a meal was provided for them and handed round by young lamas. Afterwards they were taken into the presence of the holy lama, who was attended by a dozen lesser lamas and seated at an altar on his roof-court. The British were given seats along the sides of the court opposite to him, while the porters filled up the space in the middle.

In turn the British walked up to the lama's altar and he touched each upon the head with the silver prayer wheel which he held in his left hand. The Gurkhas and porters followed and appeared to be deeply affected by the simple ceremony. The lama then delivered a short but impressive address, encouraging the men to persevere, and assuring them that he would personally pray for them. And the reverence with which the men entered and left the presence of the great lama was, says Geoffrey Bruce, eloquent testimony of his influence over them. His prayers and his blessing put fresh heart into them. And on the return journey to the Base Camp they became nearly their cheery normal selves once more.

Meanwhile, Norton and Bruce had been working out a reorganization of the porter corps. To get the most out of them they were to be made up into three definite parties, each to be led by a selected porter. The next best was to be second-in-command and take charge if anything happened to the leader. These leaders and seconds-in-command would be given extra pay and generally treated as non-commissioned officers. There was little difficulty in selecting these six men as the hardships of the past week had shown up clearly who were the most reliable. Those selected were then called up before Norton and Bruce, who explained what was expected of them, and they were then allowed, as far as possible, to choose their own men for their own parties. They seemed pleased with the idea. And the scheme had the advantage of supplying a little healthy rivalry and *esprit de party* throughout the porter corps.

Hingston also had been busy. For a day or two after the return of the expedition there were many sick to attend to. On the following morning he and Bruce had set out with a stretcher to bring in Shamsher, as he thought the only hope for the poor man was to bring him down to a lower altitude. With the utmost care he was carried down from Camp I, but was unable to last out the journey and died half a mile from the Base Camp. A few days later, Manbahadur, the cobbler, also died. Even if he had lived he would have lost both feet below the ankle. They were both buried in a sheltered spot, and their names, together with the names of the others who succumbed during the three expeditions, were inscribed on the monument which was subsequently erected near the Base Camp. Shamsher's loss was particularly to be regretted, for he was, in the words of Geoffrey Bruce, 'a gallant and loyal young man, who had worked with the most conspicuous and whole-hearted zeal throughout'.

The day after the lama had given his blessing was a brilliantly fine day without a cloud in the sky and the mountain looked clear and serene. The weather seemed settled and it was decided to make a fresh start upward on the following day, May 17th – the very day that had originally been fixed for the final assault upon the mountain. And a new programme had been worked out by Mallory, showing the movements of each climber and each party of porters for the next ten days, the intention being to put the original scheme in motion again but with the date of the final attempt on the summit put back from May 17th to May 29th. It was running the monsoon very fine, but there was no help for it.

As a preliminary move, the Gurkha NCOs and a small party left the base on the evening of the 16th and reoccupied Camp I so that there should be no delay in making a real start on the morrow.

All were hopeful that now, at last, things would improve. But on the very morning of the start the first new blow came. Beetham was down with an acute attack of sciatica, and could scarcely move. He had recovered from his dysentery and by sheer exertion of will had made himself fit to come on with the expedition. Now he was completely knocked up. It was a serious matter, for, apart from his irrepressible zeal, his skill and experience in mountaineering would be sorely needed ahead. There were none too many climbers as it was.

With this exception, however, there was no hitch in the march up the glacier, and by the evening of May 19th the expedition was in full occupation of it up to Camp III. Norton, Somervell, Mallory and Odell were at Camp III; Irvine and Hazard at Camp II, en route for Camp III; Noel and Geoffrey Bruce at Camp I, en route for Camp II; and Hingston and Beetham at the Base Camp. Weather conditions appeared to be much more favourable. There was a certain amount of cloud about the mountain, but, on the whole, the days had been bright and sunny.

The North Col, the principal obstacle on the way to the summit, had now to be tackled and a safe way made to Camp IV. Being composed wholly of ice, more or less covered with snow, its cracks and rents and crevasses varied with each year and had to be investigated anew on each expedition. And after the loss of seven porters in the avalanche in 1922 the North Col had to be approached with becoming caution this time. Moreover, it was not a matter of a few skilled climbers ascending it: a way had to be found by which laden porters could go up and down in confidence. The Sherpa porters were good fellows but not practised mountaineers. With good hard snow where nails can grip, with steps cut clean and clear by a climber on any ice slope, with a handrail here and there at danger points, and with the assurance that at the end of the day they will find good food and a warm bed, they will, says Mallory, go up and down steep tracks without a qualm, happy, confident and safe. But the fewest inches of snow enormously increase the labour of carrying a load up the North Col. All that before was firm and sure becomes slippery and uncertain. Instead of stepping confidently with body erect the porters crawl hesitatingly on, hugging the slope. All sense of security is gone. And this year there was more snow and greater cold than in 1922. The porters had already suffered severely from the cold, and the additional snow on the North Col made it all the more necessary to prepare a good way for them.

With this intention a strong party of climbers set out from Camp III on May 20th, and Norton, thinking that Mallory, who was suffering from a 'high altitude' throat, and Somervell, who had a touch of the sun, might not be able to go on, joined the party himself. It now consisted of those three and Odell, together with Lhakpa Tsering carrying a load of Alpine rope and pickets for the more difficult places. Their pace was very slow at first and it soon became apparent that Somervell was suffering from more than the usual lassitude. He had, in fact, a rather severe attack of sunstroke. He was intent on struggling on, but Norton and Mallory forcibly persuaded him to return, and he went back to camp thoroughly disgusted.

What Norton and Mallory had now to do was to find a way which would be clear of avalanches. They could see an immense crevasse stretching right across the face of the great ice slopes of the North Col. The slopes up to the crevasse though steep were safe, and the crevasse itself would be a barrier against avalanches from higher up. So they would make for this crevasse and then work along its lower lip till they found a safe way to the ledge or shelf on the North Col on which a camp could be established.

The crevasse, then, was the first point to make for. Norton and Mallory going on together ahead of Odell and the laden porter, shared the laborious work of cutting or stamping steps in the series of slightly convex snow slopes, mostly lying at a comparatively gentle angle, which gave access to the right end of the crevasse. Two minor crevasses were encountered; and the last pitch up to the big crevasse was steep, showing that a fixed rope would there be required for the porters. But the big crevasse was reached with no more serious drawback than the labour of cutting steps. It was a different matter, however, now the crevasse itself had to be tackled. There was no easy way along its lower lip, for it was broken halfway across. And the break in the lip required very careful negotiation. A descent had to be made into the bottom of the crevasse and from there they would have to climb out again by what looked like a nearly vertical wall of broken ice leading up to a narrow crack or chimney which formed the only means of access to the lower lip again beyond the break.

This was the situation which confronted Norton and Mallory as they stood on the edge of the crevasse. In order to get along the lower lip they must somehow negotiate this nasty break in it. And the only way to do this was to descend into the crevasse and climb the wall and chimney.

'Confronted with a formidable climbing obstacle,' says Norton, 'Mallory's behaviour was always characteristic: you could positively see his nerves tighten up like fiddle strings. Metaphorically he girt up his loins, and his first instinct was to jump into the lead. Up the wall and chimney he led here, climbing carefully, neatly, and in that beautiful style that was all his own.' Norton backed him up, affording him every now and then foothold with haft or head of his axe. The wall, like most ice walls, was not so steep as it looked, and required only careful step-cutting. The chimney was the facer. The snow in the bed of it gave no foothold and seemed to conceal a bottomless crack. Its sides were of smooth blue ice, and were so close together that steps could not be cut in them. The climb up this chimney was as steep and difficult as one could wish to find on any big mountain, says Mallory. It was just a gymnastic exercise which would have been severe enough at ordinary levels but exhausting nearly to the limit at 22,000 feet.

From the chimney they emerged on to a welcome little

platform and were now on the other side of the big break in the lower lip of the main crevasse. Along this lower lip they now continued their way with the crevasse on the right-hand side and a steep slope on the left. The way was safe from avalanches but steep, and more step-cutting was necessary. Then, beyond the far extremity of the crevasse, came more trouble. Norton and Mallory were now on steep snow slopes culminating in a piece about two hundred feet in height at about the extreme angle on which snow could lie and falling away at the bottom in a great ice cliff. This for the sake of convenience may be called 'the final 200 feet'.

It was the really dangerous part of the climb. It did not require gymnastic exertion like the chimney, but it represented a greater danger. The whole surface snow might peel off and carry the climbers into the abyss below. In 1921, indeed, the surface had thus peeled off in the interval between Mallory's climb up it and his subsequent descent. On the present occasion Mallory's nerves responded as usual to the call on them and he again insisted on taking the lead. To diminish the danger as much as possible it was decided to climb nearly vertically up the steepest pitch and only traverse to the left at its top when the slope began to ease off towards the edge of the shelf above – the shelf or ledge which was to be used as the site of Camp IV. Odell had now joined Norton and Mallory and he and Norton prepared to hold Mallory from below from a safe corner by a serac if the treacherous surface should slip and carry him past them. No such misfortune happened, and half an hour later they each followed in turn up the steep ladder of steps which Mallory had cut with such labour in the half-ice, half-snow surface.

They were then on the shelf, still bathed in sunshine and pleasantly sheltered from the terrible west wind by a wall of ice. No sign of the old 1922 camp could be found, for the whole jumble of snow hummocks and ice cliffs was part of a true glacier and consequently on the move. And the shelf itself was narrower than in 1922. It now formed a hog-backed ridge of untrodden, glistening snow barely affording level space enough for the row of little six-feet square tents that would be erected there.

It had been an exhausting climb as every footstep of the way had been kicked or cut with an axe to leave a clear and safe way for the porters to follow next day. But they were pleased at having established once more the most difficult portion of the whole route up the mountain. And Odell and Mallory had still sufficient energy left to prospect the way from the ledge on to the actual col, while Norton drove pickets for a fixed rope which would hang down the steepest part of the ladder of steps leading up this final 200 feet.

Mallory was exhausted with all his previous step-cutting and Odell now took the lead. The site of Camp IV is separated from the actual col by a maze of snow ridges and partially concealed crevasses, and through it a way had to be found. Odell happily succeeded in finding a bridge across the most serious crevasse; and a feasible route was established. This put the finishing touch to a good day's work, and at 3.45 they started down.

But they were thoroughly exhausted men and from sheer weariness allowed themselves to run risks they would, in an ordinary way, have carefully avoided. They took the old 1922 route and went fast. Norton and Mallory were on ahead unroped. Odell and the porter followed behind. First Norton had a nasty slip. Then the porter slipped, and having tied the rope on to himself with only a reef knot the rope came undone and he was only saved from fatal consequences by a lucky patch of soft snow. And now Mallory himself was in serious trouble. He had walked into an obvious crevasse. He had prodded the snow with which it was choked and had thought he was safe. But the snow suddenly gave way and in he went, falling about ten feet before he fetched up breathless and half blind; for the snow had tumbled all round him as he fell, and he had gone through some nasty moments before he found himself precariously supported by the ice axe which he still held in his right hand and which had caught across the crevasse. It was lucky it had, for beneath him was an unpleasant black hole.

At first he was afraid to make efforts to extricate himself lest more loose snow should fall in on him and bury him. But up through the round hole which he had made in the fall he could see the blue sky; so he shouted for help. It was in vain. His shouts were not heard, and his fall had not been seen, for he was on ahead and those behind had troubles of their own. All he could do now was to clamber out with his own efforts. With the greatest caution he set to work bringing the snow down, little by little, making at the same time a hole towards the side. Then by careful climbing he managed to extricate himself from his horrible position and at last stood on the slope once more. But he was now on the wrong side of the crevasse, and he had to cut steps across a nasty slope of very hard ice and further down some mixed unpleasant snow before he was really safe. And that cutting against time, after such a day, brought him to about the limit of his endurance.

He eventually joined his companions and they proceeded together to Camp III all a good deal ashamed of themselves at having let their weariness make them so careless. But even at night Mallory got no proper rest. His throat for some days past had been bad, and now he had fits of coughing which tore him in pieces and made sleep impossible. Headache he had, too, and general misery. The others were not much better. They could only console themselves with the thought that at any rate they had pioneered the way up this most serious obstacle. The turn for others to take up the burden had come.

Chapter Twenty-Two

THE RESCUE

The way having been prepared by Norton and Mallory the actual establishment of Camp IV on the North Col was the next step to be taken. The task was entrusted to Somervell, Hazard and Irvine. And, as time was pressing, and the monsoon might shortly be on, a start was made on May 21st, the day after Norton and Mallory had marked out the way up. Somervell was – or pretended he was – better, and with the other two climbers and twelve porters carrying tents, stoves and provisions he was to establish Camp IV on the shelf selected by Norton. He was to help the porters up the chimney and fix ropes in the worst places, particularly that nasty final 200 feet just below the shelf, and was to return with Irvine the same day, leaving Hazard and the twelve porters in the newly established camp. Then Odell and Geoffrey Bruce were to follow on May 22nd, sleep that night at Camp IV, and on the 23rd go on with the porters and establish Camp V.

It was a simple plan but trouble arose at once. The morning of May 21st was unduly warm with a lot of light cloud about. Soon soft wet snow began to fall. The tracks which Norton and Mallory had cut out or stamped with such trouble had been obliterated. The snow was deep. The going was laborious. And the climbers had to drive in pickets and fix ropes in the worst places for the porters following behind them. The worst part of all was the 'chimney'. Up such a place men could hardly carry loads. Another expedient had to be tried. Close by was a vertical ice cliff. Loads could be hauled up that in one pull from the bottom to a little platform at the top, enabling the porters to go up the chimney unladen. So Somervell and Irvine took their stand on the platform and pulled the loads up, while Hazard remained at the base of the wall superintending operations. The strain on Somervell and Irvine was severe, and an obtruding bulge added to their difficulties; but one by one they hauled up the twelve loads varying from twenty to thirty pounds each. And having seen Hazard and the twelve porters on to the shelf where they were to pitch camp – pitch it with heavy snow still falling – they themselves returned to Camp III, reaching it at 6.35 p.m. It had been a gruelling day's work, but the camp was set up.

That was on May 21st. Snow fell all night, and it was snowing hard the next morning, and it continued to snow till 3 p.m. Geoffrey Bruce and Odell could not therefore start for the North Col.

The snow had ceased in the afternoon but the cold rapidly increased. That night – May 22nd–23rd – the thermometer fell to minus 24 degrees Fahrenheit. And minus 24 degrees at 21,000 feet is a very different thing from minus 24 degrees at sea level. And minus 24 degrees in a nasty little tent where you have to sleep on the ground is a very different thing from minus 24 degrees when you look at it outside through the windows of a comfortable house. Much lower temperatures are of course recorded from many parts of the world. But on few occasions can this low temperature be so hard to bear as the cold which these Everest climbers had to endure. On the Tibet Mission the cold was hard enough to bear, but then it only fell to minus 18 degrees and the altitude was only 15,000 feet, and officers, at least, had beds to sleep on. Those therefore who have experienced great cold at great heights will appreciate best what Norton and his companions went through at this time.

May 23rd broke cloudless, windless and brilliantly fine, though the air was keen as a knife. And this gave promise that the fresh fallen snow on the slopes of the North Col would be safe. Geoffrey Bruce and Odell were, accordingly, allowed to proceed with their programme and started at 9.30 with seventeen porters.

But what about Hazard and his twelve porters all this time? They had been left on the North Col on May 21st. Snow had fallen nearly all May 22nd. The night between that and May 23rd had been the coldest on record in these parts. Their camp was not on moraine like Camp III, but on snow – and it was 2000 feet higher. What about them all this time? It was a matter of deep concern to Norton. And it was a relief to him just before one, when it began to snow steadily again and nothing more was visible, to see rows of little black dots like flies on a whitewashed wall slowly moving downward from Camp IV. They must be Hazard's party coming back to Camp III, and he was glad of it.

Geoffrey Bruce and Odell later on – about three o'clock – he saw returning too, together with their porters. They had reached a point where the snow was in a dangerous condition and they had seen Hazard's party above them descending the chimney, so they concluded that it would be wise to return.

Hazard's arrival was, therefore, now awaited with great anxiety. He reached Camp at about five o'clock. But he came with only eight men; four had been left behind. They were unable to face that dangerous slope, the 'final 200 feet' just under the shelf on which Camp IV is placed. Hazard had gone first to test the condition of the fresh surface snow. Eight men had followed him. But the last four had turned back. Perhaps they were sick – certainly two of them were frostbitten. More probably one of them had started a patch of the surface snow slipping and they had been afraid to come on: they would not be likely to forget what had happened a little further down on these same slopes during the last expedition.

Whatever the cause, there they were stranded on the North Col. And now the snow was falling persistently and in the form of soft feathery flakes rendering the passage up to or down from the col increasingly dangerous.

What should be done, Norton does not seem to have doubted for a moment. Some men might have hesitated. Some might have thought the position irretrievable. Not so Norton. He might justifiably have argued with himself that the weather was too hopelessly bad for anyone to venture on those ice slopes. It would be sad to leave the poor men to their fate. Still he must consider the lives of others as well as theirs and must consider also the object of the whole expedition. If he sent out a rescue expedition they also might lose their lives. And if they did not actually lose their lives they might be so exhausted by the effort that they would be useless for any extreme effort on the mountain later, and the chance of reaching the top might be gone.

Norton might very reasonably have so argued with himself.

But he did not reason at all. He instinctively acted. All along, his one fixed determination had been that on no account must there be any casualties among the porters this year. There was only one thing to do and that was to rescue them. They must be got down alive at all costs. Further, he himself must be of the rescue party – he and two others, and the two very best climbers, Mallory and Somervell. Only the best would do for this work. And this decision he came to – and the other two equally with himself contributed to it – although they were all three ill from their exhausting experiences at this 21,000-feet camp, and from their arduous work in pioneering the way up the North Col.

At the risk of his own life, at the risk of Mallory's and Somervell's lives, these men must be rescued. They were of a different race and of a different religion and of only a lowly position in life. But they were fellow-men. More, they were fellow-men in a common adventure. They were ever ready to risk their lives for their leaders. Their leaders must now risk their lives for them.

Fellowship told. And this sense of fellowship must have been deeply ingrained in the very texture of Norton, Somervell and Mallory, for in their present condition of cold and misery and illness, when life was flickering but faintly within them, it would be only the deepest promptings that would survive. All the superficial would have vanished long before. Unless this sense of fellowship was a root disposition with them, unless they could feel their fellows at home expecting of them that they should behave as men, nothing would have been seen of it now.

Yet all three were fully alive to the risks they were running. Mallory and Somervell had very bad coughs and sore throats which would, they knew, hamper them badly in climbing. Norton himself was, according to Mallory, not really fit to start. And the weather continued bad. Snow was still pattering on their tent as they sat in conclave. And Mallory writes that with this snow about it looked 10 to 1 against their getting up, let alone getting a party down. He himself had experience of being buried in an avalanche on this North Col, and of falling down a crevasse.

Luckily the snow stopped falling at midnight; and at 7.30 the next morning, May 24th, they were off. And when they got on to the slopes of the North Col they found the snow was not so very bad, as there had been no time for it to get sticky. It was heavy going though – hard treadmill work with the snow anything from a foot to waist deep, and they were half sick with the cold and the altitude. They drove themselves somehow or other over the fresh snow of the glacier basin and then up and up, slowly and wearily, puffing and coughing. Mallory led at first. Then Somervell took them up to where Geoffrey Bruce and Odell had dumped their loads the day before. Afterwards Norton, who had crampons – contrivances with sharp spikes fitted to the boot – assumed the lead and was able to take the party without step-cutting up to the big crevasse where they halted for half an hour. About 1.30 they were at the foot of the wall below the chimney. Every step was filled with snow. But there remained the thin descending line of rope fixed by Somervell, and grasping it with both hands they pulled themselves up the chimney. On two other dangerous sections Norton and Somervell in turn went ahead on the long rope, while the remaining two secured them. Then they came to the very dangerous 'final 200 feet' and on the shelf at the top they could see one of the marooned porters standing on the edge. Norton shouted to him asking if they were fit to walk. The answering query came, 'Up or down?' 'Down, you fool,' was the reply. And he disappeared to fetch his three companions.

Up to this point the condition of the snow had proved less dangerous than they had expected, but at the final traverse evidently presented real danger. This dangerous slope Somervell insisted on going across first, while Norton and Mallory prepared to belay the 200 feet of rope which they had brought with them for emergencies. They drove both their ice axes up to their heads into the snow as a holdfast. And round these ice axes they passed the rope, paying it out yard by yard as Somervell laboriously made his way upwards and across the steep ice slope, punching big safe steps as he went.

He was getting nearer and nearer to the four men waiting on the crest of the slope, but when he had almost reached them he had come to the end of his tether – to the end of the rope which was holding him. He was still ten yards short of the men. What now should be done? It was four o'clock, and time was pressing. The climbers quickly decided that the men must chance the unbridged ten yards. They must come separately across the dangerous part and each as he reached Somervell would be passed across the taut rope to Norton and Mallory.

The first two reached Somervell safely. One of these reached Norton, and the second was just starting, when the snow gave beneath the remaining two – stupidly coming over together – and in an instant they were flying down the slope. For one paralysing moment Norton figured them shooting over the edge of the blue ice cliff, 200 feet below. But they suddenly pulled up. They had hit upon snow bound by the cold of morning and the sun of midday to a holding consistency. They were told to sit still where they were while Somervell, as cool as a cucumber, first passed the second man on along the rope to Norton and then paid attention to their unfortunate companions.

The rescue of these two in their dreadful plight now needed the very acme of mountaineering skill. First Somervell had to restore the men's nerves, so he chaffed them till they almost laughed. Then he drove his ice axe up to its head into the soft snow, untied the rope from his waist, passed it round the axe and strained it so as to make every foot of it tell, while Norton and Mallory held their end at extreme arm's length. Having thus made the most of the rope he let himself down to its furthest length, and, holding on to the end of it with one hand, stretched out the other arm till he could just touch one of the men. Then grasping him securely by the scruff of the neck he hauled him up to the anchorage of the ice axe. The second he treated in the same way. And the rescue was effected.

The wretched pair were back in comparative safety, but their nerves were so shaken that they slid and slipped as they went along the rope to the haven of Norton and Mallory, and only saved themselves from further disaster by means of the rope handrail. When at last they were safely across, Somervell again tied the rope round his waist and followed. And a fine object lesson in mountain craft it was, says Norton, to see him, balanced and erect cross the ruined track without a slip or mistake.

A race with darkness now began, for it was 4.30 when they started down. Mallory led with one porter on a rope. Somervell followed, shepherding two others. Norton brought up the rear with a porter whose hands were cruelly frostbitten and quite useless, and whose whole weight he had to bear in places such as the chimney.

By 7.30 p.m. as they were leaving the ice slopes of the North Col and were three-quarters of a mile from home ('home,' Norton calls it, but it was only Camp III), figures loomed up out of the darkness ahead and they found Noel and Odell waiting for them with hot soup. Once more Noel had come in just when most wanted.

The climbers had rescued the four men, but the three were exhausted men. Somervell all the time that he had been punching those steps across the slope had been coughing and choking in the most distressing manner. Mallory's cough kept him awake all that night. And Norton's feet were very painful. The three had saved the porters' lives, but at what cost to themselves they were to discover later on when only a thousand feet from their goal.

After such experiences the expedition was in no condition to proceed at once with the assault on Everest. A second retirement down the glacier to the lower camps for recuperation was imperative. And already Norton had directed the retirement to begin while he and his companions were rescuing the marooned porters. To turn their backs once more on the mountain and just at the moment when the monsoon might be expected was a bitter blow. But there was no help for it. Not a single member was fit to go on in his present condition. The cold and the strenuous exertions had broken down the party for the moment – especially the best climbers, upon whom the brunt had chiefly fallen. A few days' rest at lower altitudes was a necessity.

Geoffrey Bruce, Hazard and Irvine, with most of the porters, had already proceeded down the glacier; and the day after the rescue Norton and the rest followed. They were a miserable little party of the lame and the blind, and they had to make their way to Camp II in the teeth of a north-east snowstorm. On the following day, May 26th, Norton and Somervell reached Camp I and the party was now disposed as follows: Odell, Noel and Shebbeare remained at Camp II with some twenty porters; Mallory, Somervell, Bruce and Irvine were with Norton at Camp I; Hazard had gone through to the base, where he had joined Hingston and Beetham.

The object in thus stringing out the party in echelon was to enable it to resume operations with the minimum of delay when the weather should be favourable. Those intended for the next advance to the North Col were at Camp II, so that when once the word was given they could reoccupy Camp IV with only one day's delay.

The same afternoon that they arrived at Camp I another council of war was held, ways and means were examined, and a new and simpler plan made. And when the transport question was investigated a very serious position was disclosed. Shebbeare and Bruce agreed that out of the fifty-five porters originally available only *fifteen* could now be counted on. The number physically disabled was small; but the extreme cold, coming in addition to the high altitude effects, had taken the heart out of them and they could no longer be relied on. And so far little had been done. Camp IV had barely been established with four tents and sleeping bags for twelve porters and one climber. All the food and fuel had still to be carried up there, as well as every oxygen apparatus and cylinder that would be required on the mountain, and all the tents and stoves for the higher camps. And Camp V had also to be established and stocked – and according to the original plan fifteen porters would be required for that alone.

The question of time had also to be considered. They were now within six days of the date on which the monsoon broke in 1922. Two or three days' rest would be required and one more day would be wasted getting to Camp III. The plan must obviously be such as would enable the climbers to stage a serious attempt on the summit with the least possible delay once they again advanced to the assault.

The oxygen question also again arose. There was doubt whether those who had already used it had derived any real benefit from it.

The council of war was long and indecisive, and Norton summoned a fuller council for the next day, inviting Odell, Shebbeare and Hazard to join from Camp II and the base. At this second council every possible combination of the seven available climbers was thought out, and the whole matter in every detail considered. Eventually the simplest possible plan was adopted. The oxygen was to be scrapped, and a series of assaults by pairs of climbers was to be made. The pairs would leave Camp IV on consecutive fine days and sleep two nights above that camp, once at Camp V at about 25,500 feet, and once at Camp VI at about 27,200 feet. And Norton insisted on there always being a supporting party of two climbers at Camp IV.

In allocating the climbers to these various parties Norton stipulated that Mallory had the right to join the first party if he wished. His throat was markedly better, and though he had so far borne the brunt of the hardest work, yet, says Norton, the energy and fire of the man were reflected in his every gesture, and none doubted his fitness to go as high as any. Of the remainder Bruce was now palpably the strongest. So Mallory and Bruce were to form the first pair. Somervell's throat was still far from right; but it was benefiting a little by the warmth of Camp I, his prestige since 1922 was enormous, and his rescue of the marooned porters had enhanced it. He was to be one of the second pair. The choice of the second member was left to Somervell and Mallory, Norton again leaving it to them to choose between himself, Odell, Irvine and Hazard. They chose Norton, and in making their choice they had to consider the importance of having with each party a climber who could talk sufficient Nepalese to carry the porters with him when their resolution might begin to flag. Odell and Irvine were to be supporters at Camp IV, and Hazard was to remain at Camp III.

May 28th, like the 27th, was cloudlessly fine and hot, and some ardent spirits wanted to be at the mountain again. But Norton was so impressed with the improvement in the general health that he decided to remain for yet another day. It was not wasted: the fifteen 'Tigers', as they were nicknamed, were collected at Camp II, and Odell and Irvine made up a rope ladder of Alpine rope and tent pegs to enable loaded porters to climb the steep ice wall below the chimney on the North Col.

On May 30th the final move forward began. The climbing parties, accompanied by Noel and his cinema outfit, reached Camp III.

Chapter Twenty-Three

THE ASSAULT

The great moment had now arrived. Twice the climbers had been rebuffed by snow and cold and wind. For the third time they now returned to the assault. And this time the weather was almost perfect. They themselves were exhausted and reduced in numbers; but the blizzards were over; day after day the mountain stood out sharp and clear; and the climbers were eager to seize the last opportunity before the monsoon should break, smother the whole mountain in snow, and make climbing impossible.

Being human, each climber would naturally have wished that he himself might be in the first of the successive pairs of climbers which would carry out the assault. The mountain might be carried at the first assault and the other pairs not have a chance. Or, even if the first pair failed, the monsoon or some tempest, might prevent more than one pair making an attempt. The odds were on the first pair. And Norton as the leader might very well have put himself in the first pair. But as we have seen he had chivalrously stood down. Not his own personal fame but the success of the whole expedition was the one and only thing he had in mind now at the climax as it had been from the first. Every little act that would contribute towards success was to be done. Every little act that might foil success was to be shunned. So now it was to be Mallory and Geoffrey Bruce, who at the moment seemed to be palpably the strongest of the climbers, who were to make the first assault and it was hoped gain the great prize.

They set off from Camp III on June 1st, taking with them nine of the 'Tigers'. The weather was again perfect and they were full of hope. On their way to the North Col they fixed the rope ladder on the ice wall below the chimney in the crevasse so as to make things easier for laden porters. And on arrival at Camp IV they found Odell and Irvine already established there prepared to fulfil the function of supporters, attend to the comfort of exhausted climbers after an assault, have warm meals ready, and succour returning parties of porters.

On June 2nd Mallory and Geoffrey Bruce with their nine porters set out for the real assault on the mountain. They hoped to establish Camp V the first day, Camp VI the second, and be on the summit the third. And it was not an unreasonable hope, for the weather conditions remained perfect, the sky was clear and there were no signs yet of the monsoon. Alas! in the Himalaya a bright sun and a clear sky as a rule mean wind. Between the heated plains and the icy peaks strong currents of air are set in motion. And no sooner had Mallory's party got outside the shelter of the ice blocks on the North Col than they were struck with the full blast of the raging air sweeping on the mountain from the north-west. The party was provided with windproof clothing, but it was of no more avail than are 'waterproofs' against tropical rain. The wind tore through windproof garments, through woollen garments, through the very flesh, right into the bones. It penetrated everything. And it not only penetrated: it exerted pressure. Laden porters could scarcely keep their foothold against it.

Norton describes the mountain above North Col as 'an easy rock peak with no ice or crevasses'. But he was addressing the Alpine Club when he used the word 'easy' and the Alpine Club speak in a different language from the rest of the world. The mountain may be easy in this language, but it must obviously be steep or snow would be lying on it. And how steep it is we can gather from the fact that whenever we hear of a climber dropping anything we also invariably hear that it has disappeared. Through this tearing wind the party had to make their way up the steep rocky face edge of Everest.

Camp V was to have been established on the east or sheltered side of the ridge at about 25,300 feet. But at about 25,000 feet the porters became exhausted. (It is well again to remind ourselves that before the Everest expedition 24,600 feet was the highest altitude attained by any man, even unladen.) Only four porters were game. The remainder had deposited their loads, unable to come on. Mallory had to stop, therefore, and organize a camp while Geoffrey Bruce and the sturdy Lobsang went back twice and carried up the missing loads on their own backs. It was a gallant effort – for Lobsang, because he had already carried his own load up; and for Bruce, because he had not, like the porters, been accustomed all his life to carrying loads on mountains – or anywhere else.

'Two fragile little tentlets perched on an almost precipitous slope', in Norton's words, now were dignified with the style and title of Camp V. Five porters, according to plan, were returned to the North Col supporting camp and three of the best were kept to carry on one more tent to form a camp 2000 feet higher.

The next morning, June 3rd, Mallory and Bruce should have set out for the summit. But even over night they had not been hopeful of the men. The wind had entered not only their bones but their hearts. It had chilled all the spirit in them. And next morning neither Bruce nor Mallory could make anything of them. One was ready to go on. The other two professed themselves sick. Geoffrey Bruce, like his older cousin General Bruce, has a great way with these hill men. But nothing even he could do could stir them. Moreover, Bruce himself was suffering the penalty of carrying those loads on the previous day, and his heart was strained. There was nothing for it but to return to the North Col. The first attempt, upon which the expedition had counted so much, had failed.

Now as Mallory and Bruce were leaving Camp V downward, Norton and Somervell, timed to follow them a day behind, were leaving Camp IV upward. And the parties met in between the two camps. The sight of Mallory coming back was a nasty blow to Norton. It meant one less chance of reaching the summit. It *might* mean also that no porters at all would be able to carry a camp any higher than 25,000 feet, and this would mean an end of every chance. It was a bad lookout. However, while Mallory and Bruce pursued their way downward to the North Col, there to be welcomed and refreshed by Odell and Irvine, who were now the very valuable supporting party on which Norton, after his own experience in 1922, set so much store, Norton and Somervell proceeded upward. They, too, experienced the biting Everest wind. But they were able to reach Camp V and there they kept four of their porters in the hopes that on the morrow they would be willing to carry one tent to about the 27,000-feet level. These four porters had to sleep in one of the tents fixed by Mallory, while the two climbers slept in the other. Norton and Somervell found the floor of their tent had been well-levelled by their predecessors and, after making a good meal of pemmican and 'bully' beef, coffee and biscuits, they spent a fair night, sleeping at least half of it – and this latter is an important point, for it had formerly been supposed that sleep at so high an altitude would be impossible.

The crux, however, was whether the porters would or would not go on the next day. Norton says he had gloomy forebodings that night: there was nothing whatever in the attitude of the porters to encourage him to hope that he and Somervell would next day succeed any better than Mallory and Bruce in getting men to carry loads higher. On the following morning the two climbers rose at five o'clock to tackle the problem, and the next few hours were one of the great turning points in the history of Everest exploration. If these porters, as well as Mallory's, proved to be unfit or unwilling to go on, not only would the expedition end in failure but any future expedition would be discouraged: they would almost take it for granted that porters could not carry loads beyond 25,000 feet.

If we are to understand what men are like at five o'clock in the morning on the face of Mount Everest we must recall what bees are like on a cold autumn morning. Ordinarily these busy little bees are full of life and activity. Now they can scarcely move; they are numbed; they have neither energy nor intelligence; the spring of being is almost gone out of them. The porters were just like that, and probably Norton himself was not very much livelier. When he got down to the men's tent groans were the only answer he got to his questions. But he then did a very wise thing. He induced them to cook and eat a meal, and he went back and had some breakfast himself. After breakfast things look better than they do before. On an empty stomach all things seem impossible. Certainly, carrying loads up Mount Everest would. After breakfast even that might be considered.

All having fed, Norton addressed himself to the task. The struggle which now ensued between him and the four porters was essentially a struggle of spirit. All that organization could do had been done. Thought could do no more. It was simply a question whether spirit could be induced to drive the body any further. And this depended not so much upon will power as upon imagination. And here again Norton showed wisdom. He appealed to the imagination: and it is by the imagination that we are all carried along on great enterprises. There was no holding a pistol to their heads; no physical force; no threats; nor even bribing by money. He simply painted for the porters a picture of themselves covered with honour and glory and receiving praises from everyone; and he told them how their names would be inscribed in letters of gold in the book which would be written to describe their achievement if only they would carry loads to 27,000 feet. It was a master stroke. The appeal was made straight to their manhood. 'Show yourselves men and you will be honoured by men,' was in effect what Norton said. And Norton and Somervell could make the appeal, for they had shown themselves men and good comrades by the way in which they had gone back at great risk to their lives, their health, and the success of the whole expedition, to rescue those four porters marooned on the North Col. To their everlasting honour the porters now responded. Three, at least, did: the other was really too ill. Their names my readers should turn into gold as they read them. They are:

NAPBOO YISHAY
LHAKPA CHEDI
SEMCHUMBI

The critical point had been turned and an advance instead of a retreat was made. And once they were off the men went well – though Semchumbi, through suffering from a blow on the knee, went somewhat lame and had to be shepherded by Somervell who was himself feeling his throat very badly, and had constantly to stop and cough. The easy scree of the first day's climb became looser as they climbed higher, and energy as well as temper suffered, says Somervell, in the weary plod from 25,000 to 26,800 feet, when the scree gives place to sloping slabs covered with small stones, which render footing precarious. And halts were needed to help them to keep breathing sufficiently to meet their bodily needs. But the weather continued fine and the wind was markedly less severe than on the day before. As they passed the highest point which they and Mallory had reached in 1922 – and which was of course by a long way the record height man had then reached – their spirits rose. They were going to camp higher still. And given another clear day and good conditions what might they not achieve!

So they progressed till about 1.30, when it was evident that the gallant Semchumbi could go no further. A narrow cleft in the rocks facing north and affording the suggestion – it was little more – of some shelter from the north-west wind, was selected. Norton set the two leading porters to scrape and pile the loose stones forming the floor of the cleft into the usual platform for a tent. On it the tiny tent for the two climbers was pitched; and this was Camp VI, 26,800 feet. A tent had been set at an altitude no less than 11,000 feet higher than the summit of Mont Blanc.

The situation was far from ideal, but it seemed the best available, and on Everest, says Somervell, you have got to take what you can get and be thankful. While Norton remarks that in two excursions up and down the whole length of the North Arête (the North Face Edge) of Mount Everest he never saw a single spot affording the 6-foot square level area on which a tent could be pitched without having to build a platform.

The diminutive 'camp' having been pitched the three porters were dispatched back to the North Col camp. They had played their part heroically and established for ever the all-important point that a tent *can* be pitched within climbable distance of the summit. And now the climbers were left alone to do *their* part.

But before they actually commenced the climb a night had to be spent in the camp and a second very important point had to be cleared up. Could men *sleep* at nearly 27,000 feet? By the next morning that question also had been answered – and answered favourably. Norton entered in his diary for that day, 'Spent the best night since I left Camp I.' Perhaps a sense of relief from anxiety about the porters had something to do with this. Anyhow there was the fact and it is one of great value. Somervell did not get so much sleep as Norton, but he records that 'when morning arrived we were well rested and untroubled by breathing and other effects of great altitudes.'

These two facts – that porters can carry a tent to near the 27,000-feet line, and that climbers can sleep there – are two of the most important results of this third expedition.

Chapter Twenty-Four

THE CLIMAX

The day which would determine failure or success had come. Before the sun set on June 4th, Norton and Somervell, or one of them, would either stand on the summit of Mount Everest or have to withdraw, once more baffled. The weather conditions were as good as they could ever be. The day was nearly windless and brilliantly fine. Alas! now that the weather was favourable the men were exhausted. They were not the men they might have been if they could have started fresh from Camp I, and come leisurely up the glacier gradually acclimatizing themselves on the way and leaving all the gruelling spade work to be done by others. Norton always did hold, before the expedition left England, that more climbers were required. And more climbers would have been sent if the susceptibilities of the Tibetan government had not to be considered. Four more climbers would have meant many more transport animals for one thing. And the Tibetan government were already suspicious of the size of these annual expeditions.

However, Norton and Somervell got up at dawn on June 4th full of hope. At the start one of those little contretemps occurred which annoy so much in travel. The cork came out of the thermos flask, the eagerly anticipated hot drink was emptied, and they had to go through the weary task of fetching and melting snow to make another hot drink. Theoretically, leaders of Everest expeditions ought to see that corks do not come out of thermos flasks. But accidents will happen in the best-regulated expeditions.

Norton and Somervell started at 6.45 and struck off to the right in a slanting direction south-westward along the North Face towards the summit, which was about a mile distant as the crow flies and 2200 feet above them. They might have struck upward and got on to the top of the ridge and followed it along but they preferred to keep under its shelter. It might have been too windy on the top. The drawback to this course was that at the start, when they most wanted the sun, they were in shade. They trudged slowly up a broad rocky shoulder making for a patch of sunlight. And at length, panting, puffing and sometimes slipping back on the scree, and so compelled to stop to regain breath, they attained the sunlight and began to get warm.

They crossed the snow patch with Norton gallantly chipping steps in front, and about an hour from camp reached the bottom edge of the broad yellow band of rock which is such a conspicuous feature in distant views of the mountain. It is about a thousand feet in thickness and afforded the climbers a safe and easy route as they traversed it diagonally, for it is made up of a series of broad ledges, some 10 feet or more wide, running parallel to its general direction and sufficiently broken up to afford easy access from one ledge to the next.

The going was good. The day was perfect. But by the time they reached the 27,500-feet level they were feeling in distress.

Norton says he felt it bitterly cold and he shivered so violently as he sat in the sun during one of their numerous halts that he suspected the approach of malaria. And yet he was wearing ample clothing – a thick woollen vest and drawers, a thick flannel shirt and two sweaters under a lightish knickerbocker suit of windproof gaberdine, the knickers of which were lined with light flannel, a pair of soft elastic Kashmir putties, and a pair of boots of felt – bound and soled with leather and lightly nailed with the usual Alpine nails, while over all he wore a very light pyjama suit of Burberry's 'Shackleton' windproof gaberdine. Fur was not worn on account of the weight. But this seemed enough to keep a man warm. To see if he really had malaria he took his pulse, and to his surprise found it about sixty-four, which was only about twenty above his normally very slow pulse.

Besides this feeling of cold Norton also at the time was beginning to experience trouble with his eyes. He was seeing double, and in a difficult step was sometimes in doubt where to put his feet.

Somervell, too, was in trouble. For some weeks he had suffered in the throat. And now the process of breathing in the intensely cold dry air, which caught the back of the larynx, had a disastrous effect on his already very bad sore throat. He had constantly to stop and cough.

The altitude was also beginning to tell upon both of them. About 27,500 feet there was an almost sudden change, says Somervell. A little lower down they could walk comfortably, taking three or four breaths for each step, but now seven, eight or ten complete respirations were necessary for each single step forward. Even at this slow rate of progress they had to indulge in a rest for a minute or two every twenty or thirty yards. Norton says that it was his ambition to do twenty consecutive paces uphill without a pause to rest and pant, elbow on bent knee. Yet he does not remember achieving it. Thirteen was nearer the mark.

About midday when they were at about the 28,000-feet level they were getting near the limit of endurance. They were just below the top edge of the yellow band and nearing the big couloir or gully which runs vertically down the mountain and cuts off the base of the final pyramid from the great North-East Ridge. Here Somervell finally succumbed to his throat trouble. As it was, he nearly died of it, and if he had gone further he certainly would have succumbed. Telling Norton that he would only hinder him if he went on, he suggested that Norton should climb the mountain by himself; and he then settled down on a sunny ledge to watch him do it.

But Norton himself was not far from the end of his tether, and could only struggle on a little further. He followed the actual top edge of the band, which led at a very slightly uphill angle into and across the big couloir. But to reach the latter he had to turn the end of two pronounced buttresses which ran down the face of the mountain. Here the going became a great deal worse. The slope below him was very steep, the foothold ledges narrowed to a few inches in width. And as he approached the shelter of the big couloir there was a lot of powdery snow which concealed the precarious footholds. The whole face of the mountain was composed of slabs like the tiles on a roof, and all sloped at much the same angle as tiles. He had twice to retrace his steps and follow a different band of strata. And the couloir itself was filled with powdery snow into which he sank to the knee, and even to the waist, and which yet was not of a consistency to support him in the event of a slip.

Beyond the couloir the going got steadily worse. He found himself stepping from tile to tile, as it were, each tile sloping smoothly and steadily downwards, and he began to feel that he was too much dependent on the mere friction of a boot nail on the slabs. It was not exactly difficult going, reports Norton, but it was a dangerous place for a single unroped climber, as one slip would, in all probability, have sent him to the bottom of the mountain.

The strain of climbing so carefully was now beginning to tell upon Norton and he was getting exhausted. In addition, his eye trouble was becoming worse and was a severe handicap. He had perhaps 200 feet more of the nasty going to surmount before he emerged on the north face of the final pyramid, to safety and an easy route to the summit. But it was now 1 p.m. His rate of progress was too slow – he had ascended only about 100 feet in a distance of perhaps 300 yards since he left Somervell – and there was no chance of his being able to climb the remaining 876 feet if he was to return in safety. So he turned back at an altitude which was subsequently fixed by theodolite observation at 28,126 feet.

Norton as well as Somervell had to give up when within only about three hours' climb of the summit. There it was, not half a mile away, but one after another they had to turn back. Immortal glory was almost within their grasp; but they were too faint to clutch it. Yet their faintness was no faint-heartedness. No stouter-hearted man or one of more indomitable courage than Somervell exists, or a more collected and persistently tenacious man than Norton. What was the true cause of their utterly coming to an end of their resources is best given in the words of their old comrade, Dr Longstaff. Longstaff, besides his ordinary professional knowledge, has also special experience in Himalayan climbing. He has himself climbed to 23,000 feet. He was with the 1922 Everest expedition up to Camp III, 21,000 feet, so, as well as knowing Norton and Somervell themselves, he knew the conditions on which they were working; and, speaking at the Alpine Club in December, 1925, he made use of these words: 'When Norton and Somervell and Mallory started up the North Col to rescue those porters they were already played out. The severe weather and labour at Camps III and IV had done them in. Their only chance was to get back quickly to the Base Camp to recover form. Instead, they had this infernally trying and excessively dangerous job of rescuing those men. That is what upset the apple-cart more than anything else. If only Somervell could have gone straight down, his throat would probably have recovered . . . Norton's double vision had nothing whatever to do with his subsequent snow-blindness: it was a symptom of derangement of the higher brain centres due to want of oxygen. But I hold that this was not due to absolute altitude so much as to the utter exhaustion produced by weeks of long-continued over-exertion just as a runner faints at the post. It's what they'd already gone through that made their pace so slow at this last shot. What they did under such conditions quite convinces me that if circumstances had been really favourable they would have got to the top.'

In short, it was the *extra* hardships which they had suffered in rescuing the porters that prevented Norton and Somervell from reaching the summit – the hardships which they had to endure in addition to their ordinary sufferings from cold and wind and snow.

By effecting the rescue they had reaffirmed that principle of loyal comradeship upon which all mountaineering must be based. But by that act they had lost the great prize which might have been theirs.

Yet this much, at least, they had done: they had shown the feasibility of climbing Mount Everest. After what they accomplished under such disadvantage it could not be doubted that under normal conditions men could reach the summit. And they had actually reached an altitude about as high as the top of Kangchenjunga – and what a stupendous height that is those thousands who have seen that world-famed mountain will know.

Everest climbers do not climb the mountain for the sake of the view. Nevertheless, we who remain below do like to know what the view was like. And it happens that both Norton and Somervell are artists. What do they say? Not very much, it is true, for in their state of physical exhaustion they were incapable of that deep feeling which is an essential element in appreciating beauty. Still their observations are of value.

Norton says: 'The view from the great height was disappointing. From 25,000 feet the wild tangle of snowy peaks and winding glaciers, each with its parallel lines of moraines like cart tracks on a snowy road, was imposing to a degree. But we were now high above the highest mountain in sight, and everything below us was so flattened out that much of the beauty of outline was lost. To the north, over the great plateau of Tibet, the eye travelled over range upon range of minor hills until all sense of distance was lost, only to be regained on picking up a row of snow peaks just appearing over the horizon like tiny teeth. The day was a remarkably clear one in a country of the clearest atmosphere in the world, and the imagination was fired by the sight of these infinitely distant peaks tucked away over the curve of the horizon.'

And Somervell writes: 'The view from the topmost points that we reached, and, indeed, all the way up, was quite beyond words for its extent and magnificence. Gyaching and Choyo, among the highest mountains in the world, were over a thousand feet beneath. Around them we saw a perfect sea of fine peaks – all giants among mountains, all as dwarfs below us. The splendid dome of Pumori, the finest of Everest's satellites, was but an incident in the vast array of peak upon peak. Over the plain of Tibet a distant range gleamed 200 miles away. The view, indeed, was indescribable, and one simply seemed to be above everything in the world and to have a glimpse almost of a god's view of things.'

A glimpse *almost* of a god's view of things, says Somervell. But what if he had actually reached the summit? So far he had seen the view of only one side and Everest still towered nearly a thousand feet above him. But from the summit he would have seen all round; his view of things would verily have been a god's. Everest itself would have been humbled beneath his feet. Man's dominion over the mountain would have been finally established. Mite as man is he would have shown that he was greater than the mountain. And far and wide he would have surveyed his domain – far over the plains of India as well as over the plains of Tibet, and east and west right along the vast array of earth's mightiest peaks, all now beneath him.

And this glory now his he would have won for himself – won largely through the efforts of others and loyalty of comrades, but won also by his own tremendous and unaided efforts. And the sight of him there in his hard-won glory on the pinnacle of the world would, he might be sure, give new heart to many another and heighten endeavour in every field.

No such vision was granted to Norton and Somervell, though they had deserved it, and had missed it only through their own devotion to their fellows. But they must have had it often in their minds as Everest first came into view when they marched across Tibet, and it must have been the ultimate incentive of all their efforts.

And now that the glory would never be theirs and they had to turn back foiled what were their feelings? Fortunately the same condition that had dulled their capacity to struggle up the final pyramid had also dulled their feelings of disappointment. Norton says that he ought to record the bitter feeling of disappointment which he should have experienced but he could not conscientiously say that he felt it much at the time. Twice he had to turn back on a favourable day when success had appeared possible, yet on neither occasion did he feel the sensations appropriate to the moment. And this he considered to be a psychological effect of great altitudes. 'The better qualities of ambition and will to conquer seem dulled to nothing, and one turns downhill with but little feeling other than relief that the strain and effort of climbing are finished.'

Yet the feeling of disappointment *did* come – and that very same day. For when they arrived back on the North Col and were welcomed by Mallory and Odell, he says, 'They kept congratulating us on having reached what we estimated as a height of 28,000 feet, though we ourselves felt nothing but disappointment at our failure.'

They were disappointed but they did not regret having made the effort, and Somervell writing on June 8th from the Base Camp says:

'We are both rather done in as regards general condition, but are satisfied that we had the weather and a good opportunity for a fight with our adversary. There is nothing to complain of. We established camps. The porters played up well. We obtained sleep even at the highest, nearly 27,000 feet. We had a gorgeous day for the climb, almost windless and brilliantly fine. Yet we were unable to reach the summit. So we have no excuse – we have been beaten in fair fight; beaten by the height of the mountain and our own shortness of breath.

'But the fight was worth it, worth it every time.'

Chapter Twenty-Five

MALLORY AND IRVINE

We now come back to Mallory. Fury raged in his soul as he was forced to return from Camp V. Fury not against the individual porters who could not be brought to go further but against the whole set of circumstances which thus compelled him to go back at the very moment when the weather at last was favourable. But Mallory was in no mind to be finally thwarted. He would recoil but to spring higher. He was absolutely possessed with the idea of climbing Mount Everest. Climbing Everest was no incident in his life. He had made it his whole life. Perhaps he had not Somervell's large geniality and way of carrying men along with him, nor Norton's capacity for leading a whole big expedition. He was more accustomed, and more fitted, to the lesser expeditions of a few choice companions. But he was more deadly intent on the *idea* than any. If any single one was the soul of the expedition it was Mallory. And his was not so much bulldog tenacity, or sheer hard determination to conquer, as the imagination of the artist who cannot leave his work until it is completely, neatly, and perfectly, finished. Mallory was himself the very embodiment of the 'Everest spirit'. And to get him away from Everest before

Everest itself had hurled him back you would have had to pull him up by the very roots of his being.

With fresh plans kindling within him he passed on from Camp IV straight through on the same day to Camp III, there to examine the possibilities of an ascent with oxygen. Mallory never was a real enthusiast for oxygen. But, if it were the only way of getting up Mount Everest, use it he would. Neither was Irvine an oxygen enthusiast, and privately he told Odell that he would rather get to the final pyramid without oxygen than to the top with it – a sentiment with which most of us will assuredly agree. And so probably would Mallory. But Mallory had this to consider – that Norton and Somervell would be doing the very utmost that the present expedition could do *without* oxygen. And, if they did not succeed, then one last attempt should be made – this time *with* oxygen. He therefore, as was his wont, threw his whole soul into the arrangements for an oxygen attempt. And he chose for his companion Irvine, not Odell, because Irvine had faith in the use of oxygen which Odell had not. Another reason was that Irvine had a genius for mechanical devising and had already worked wonders on the defective apparatus – defective because no apparatus to contain a highly condensed gas and at the same time withstand the extreme changes of temperature experienced between the plains of India and the heights of Everest, could be constructed which would not need adjustment. And a third reason, and perhaps important as any, was that Irvine had originally been allotted to him to form one of the pairs for the ascent, and Mallory had instilled him with his ideas, and deliberately worked to make the two into a true pair, and create a keen *esprit de pair*.

In the light of subsequent experience we may doubt the wisdom of using oxygen on this attempt. The heavy apparatus was a colossal handicap. And it afterwards proved that acclimatization had much greater effect than was then supposed. Odell, who had acclimatized slowly, afterwards climbed twice to 27,000 feet – once with a 20-lb oxygen apparatus on his back, though he did not use the oxygen after 26,000 feet, finding it did him little good. If Mallory had taken Odell and had made the final attempt without oxygen it is quite legitimate to suppose that the summit might have been reached. For Odell had not gone through the trying experience of the rescue which Norton, Somervell and Mallory had; and he was probably by now quite fit to reach the summit. And, exhausted as Mallory was from the effects of the rescue, yet with a fit and experienced climber beside him, with the knowledge that 28,100 feet had already actually been reached – always a great aid to endeavour – and with his spirit to spur him on, he might have kept up with Odell to the end. Or Odell and Irvine without using oxygen might have succeeded; for neither had Irvine been strained by the rescue exertions.

All this is conjecture, though. And at the time that Mallory was making his preparations he did not know that Norton had reached 28,100 feet, or how wonderfully Odell was acclimatizing. All he knew was that, so far, Odell had *not* been acclimatizing so well as the rest. And therefore the best chance of reaching the summit seemed to be by using oxygen.

On June 3rd Mallory and Geoffrey Bruce had arrived back at Camp III straight from Camp V, and together they now examined into the possibilities of collecting sufficient porters capable of carrying up oxygen supplies to Camp VI. The men had improved in health as the result of rest and fine weather; and by dint of strong, personal persuasion, Bruce was just able to get together sufficient men. And while these negotiations were proceeding Irvine was occupied in getting the oxygen apparatus into efficient working order.

Odell at this time was with Hazard in Camp IV, while that indefatigable and determined photographer Noel was established on the North Peak, at an altitude of 23,000 feet, taking cinematograph records.

Arrangements were completed on June 3rd, and on the next day Mallory and Irvine climbed up to the North Col again with the new porters. The two climbers used oxygen and covered the distance in the fast time of two and a half hours. They were well pleased with the result, but Odell was more sceptical. Irvine's throat was already suffering much from the cold dry air, and Odell thinks that the discomfort was palpably aggravated by the use of oxygen.

Here on the North Col the new climbing party and the support was assembled. This Camp IV had, indeed, become a kind of advanced mountain base for the actual assaults on the mountain. Odell has given a description of it. Its peculiarity was that it was pitched on snow and not on rock, like the others, even the highest, no rock being available. Perched on an ice ledge it had four tents: two for sahibs and two for porters. The ledge was a shelf of névé with a greatest breadth of about 30 feet. And a high wall of ice which rose above it on the western side gave comforting protection from the chilly winds which constantly blow from that direction. But for this screen the camp could never have been occupied for so long as it was: Odell himself was there no less than eleven days – a sufficiently remarkable fact considering that only a few years ago even mountaineers like Dr Hunter Workman had thought it would not be possible to sleep at 21,000 feet.

The weather conditions at such an altitude are peculiarly interesting. On two days when the sun temperature at midday was 105 degrees, the air temperature at the same time was only 29 degrees. Odell is doubtful whether the air temperature there ever does exceed the freezing point. It is probable that the snow wastes away entirely by direct evaporation. It was consequently very dry and unconsolidated and there was never any running water.

Odell himself does not seem to have been adversely affected by these trying conditions. He says that after some degree of acclimatization his sensations were really quite normal. It was only when great exertions were required that he felt 'like nothing on earth'. Certainly the bad effect of high altitude on the mentality had been exaggerated, he thought. The speed of mental processes might be slowed down; but their capacity was not impaired.

Into this camp on the same day, June 4th, that Mallory and Irvine arrived up from Camp III, Norton and Somervell returned from their great climb. They had come straight back from their highest point, without halting at Camps V and VI. Somervell had as nearly as possible collapsed altogether in a choking fit. And Norton that night became totally blind from snow blindness. They were disappointed – and naturally so – as has already been said. But to be disappointed because you have reached *only* 28,100 feet is surely a remarkable confirmation of Einstein's theory of relativity! Only recently men who had reached an altitude as high as this camp to which Norton and

Somervell had now *descended* 5000 feet were looked upon as heroes.

However, there was the fact that they had not got to the *top*, and here was Mallory, with steam at high pressure, ready to make one last desperate effort. Norton entirely agreed with this decision, and was 'full of admiration for the indomitable spirit of the man, determined, in spite of his already excessive exertions, not to admit defeat while any chance remained'. And such was Mallory's will power and nervous energy that he seemed to Norton entirely adequate to the task. All Norton differed with him about was as to taking Irvine as his companion. Irvine was suffering from throat trouble and was not the experienced climber that Odell was. Moreover, Odell though he had acclimatized slowly was beginning to show that he was a climber of unequalled endurance and toughness. But, as Mallory had completed his plans, Norton, very rightly, made no attempt at that late stage to interfere with them.

Mallory halted one day, June 5th, in camp with Norton, now in great pain from his snow blindness. And on the 6th he set out with Irvine and four porters. Who can tell his feelings? Certainly he well knew the dangers, and he set out in no rash, foolhardy spirit. This was his third expedition to Mount Everest; at the end of the first he had written that the highest of mountains is capable of 'a severity so awful and so fatal that the wiser sort of men do well to think and tremble even on the threshold of their high endeavour'; and on both the second and third expeditions he had experienced to the full the severity of Everest.

He knew the dangers before him and was prepared to meet them. But he was a man of vision and imagination as well as daring. He could see all that success meant. Everest was the embodiment of the physical forces of the world. Against it he had to pit the spirit of man. He could see the joy in the faces of his comrades if he succeeded. He could imagine the thrill his success would cause among all fellow-mountaineers; the credit it would bring to England; the interest all over the world; the name it would bring him; the enduring satisfaction to himself that he had made his life worth while. All this must have been in his mind. He had known the sheer exhilaration of the struggle in his minor climbs among the Alps. And now on mighty Everest exhilaration would be turned into exaltation – not at the time, perhaps, but later on assuredly. Perhaps he never exactly formulated it, yet in his mind must have been present the idea of 'all or nothing'. Of the two alternatives, to turn back a third time, or to die, the latter was for Mallory probably the easier. The agony of the first would be more than he as a man, as a mountaineer, and as an artist, could endure.

Irvine, younger and less experienced than Mallory, would not be so acutely aware of the risks. On the other hand, he would not so vividly visualize all that success would mean. But Odell has recorded that he was no less determined than Mallory upon going 'all out'. It had been his ambition to have 'a shot at the summit'. And now that the chance had come he welcomed it 'almost with boyish enthusiasm'.

In this frame of mind the pair set out on the morning of June 6th. The sightless Norton could only press their hands and pathetically wish them good luck. Odell and Hazard (who had come up from Camp III as Somervell had gone down) had prepared them a meal of fried sardines with biscuits and plenty of hot tea and chocolate, and at 8.40 they started. Their personal loads consisted of the modified oxygen apparatus with two cylinders only and a few other small items such as wraps and a food ration for the day, in all about 25 lb. The eight porters with them carried provisions, bedding and additional oxygen cylinders, but no oxygen apparatus for their own use.

The morning was brilliant. It clouded over in the afternoon and a little snow fell in the evening; but this was not serious and four of Mallory's porters returned in the evening from Camp V with a note saying there was no wind there and that things looked hopeful. The next morning, the 7th, Mallory's party moved on to Camp VI, while Odell came up in support to Camp V. It would have been better of course if he could have gone with them and so made a party of three. Three is the ideal number for a mountain party. But the tiny tents held only two climbers. There were not sufficient porters to carry a second tent. And he could only follow a day behind, acting as a kind of support.

Mallory made Camp VI all right with his four porters. And this fact is another evidence of the value of Norton and Somervell's work. Through *their* having got porters up to this camp, 26,800 feet, the second lot of porters with Mallory went there almost as a matter of course. And from there they were sent back with a note from Mallory to Odell saying the weather was perfect for the job, but that the oxygen apparatus was a nasty load for climbing.

That evening as Odell from Camp V looked out of his tent the weather was most promising; and he thought of the hopeful feelings with which Mallory and Irvine would go to sleep. Success would seem to be at last within their grasp.

Of what happened after that we know little. Owing to some

defect in the oxygen apparatus which required adjustment, or from some other cause, their start must have been late, for when Odell, following in rear, caught sight of them it was 12.50 p.m. and they were then only at the second rock step which, according to Mallory's schedule, they should have reached at 8 a.m. at latest. And the day had not turned out so fine as the previous evening had promised. There was much mist about the mountain. It might have been finer up where Mallory and Irvine were, for Odell looking up from below did notice that the upper part of the mist was luminous. But there was sufficient cloud about to prevent Odell from keeping in touch with the two climbers; and through the drifting mists he had only a single glimpse of them again.

As he reached the top of a little crag, at about 26,000 feet, there was a sudden clearing above him. The clouds parted. The whole summit ridge and final pyramid was unveiled. And far away on a snow slope he noticed a tiny object moving and approaching the rock step. A second object followed. And then the first climbed to the top of the step. As he stood intently watching this dramatic appearance the scene became enveloped in cloud once more. And this was the last that was ever seen of Mallory and Irvine. Beyond that all is mystery.

Chapter Twenty-Six

ODELL

Odell's movements must now be chronicled. And they are sufficiently dramatic. His role was to support Mallory and Irvine. And the day after they left the North Col he also left it with one porter and climbed to Camp V, which he had also visited once before on a day trip there and back with Hazard. But as the porter was suffering from mountain sickness, and clearly would not be available to go on the next day, Odell sent him back with the four porters who came in that afternoon from Mallory on Camp VI.

Odell was thus left completely alone in this tiny eerie at an altitude of 25,300 feet. No man has ever had such an experience, and it is one we like to dwell on. That evening, as we have seen, the weather was most promising and the outlook deeply impressive. To the westward was a wild savage jumble of peaks towering above the Rongbuk Glacier, and culminating in the mighty Cho Uyo, 26,750 feet, and Gyachungkang, 25,910 feet, bathed in pinks and yellows of most delicate tints. Right opposite were the gaunt cliffs of the North Peak, the nearness of its massive pyramid of rock only lending greater distance to the wide horizon beyond, and its dark bulk all the more exaggerating the opalescence of the far-away peaks on the northern horizon. To the eastward, floating in thin air, a hundred miles away, was the snowy summit of Kangchenjunga. Nearer was the varied outline of the Gyangkar Range.

Odell had climbed many peaks alone, and witnessed sunsets from not a few, but this, he says, was the crowning experience of all.

We may well believe it. He was in the very midst of the most awe-inspiring region on this earth. He was in the near presence of God. Revealed to him now were the might and majesty, and the purity, the calm, and the sublimity of the Great World-Spirit. And being alone, and near the very climax of a great adventure, he must have been impressionable in the highest degree, though only later in tranquillity would he be aware of the deep impress that had been made upon him.

And if the sunset was impressive so also must have been the profound and solemn stillness of the night, and the sparkling brilliance of the stars against the liquid sapphire of the sky.

And then the dawn: the first fresh radiancy of daylight, the increasing colour, the fine delicacy of hues as translucent as wine, the first flush on the peaks, the sapphire of the sky turning to the clearest azure!

Was ever a man more privileged than Odell! To behold what he beheld was to be exalted for life.

By dawn the next morning he was up. The great day, which was finally to decide the success or failure of the expedition, had arrived. Two hours were occupied in preparing his breakfast and putting on his boots – operations which at that high altitude necessitate great effort – and by eight he was off. Then, carrying a rucksack with provisions in case of shortage at Camp

VI, he made his solitary way up the steep slope of snow and ice behind Camp V till he reached the crest of the main ridge. This was a different route from that followed by Norton and Somervell, who had taken a more slanting direction along the face of the mountain, keeping well below the crest. But it was the one probably followed by Mallory. Odell did not get the glorious view – a view extending to the Tiger Hill behind Darjiling – there must be from the summit of the ridge in clear weather, for he says that, though the earlier morning had been clear and not unduly cold, the rolling banks of mist had now commenced to form and sweep across the great face of the mountain. The wind, however, fortunately for him, and for Mallory and Irvine 2000 feet above him, did not increase; and there were indications that even the mist might be confined to the lower half of the mountain. So Odell had no qualms about Mallory's progress upward from Camp VI. The wind was light and should not have hampered their progress along the crest of the ridge. And he hoped that by now Mallory and Irvine would be well on their way to the final pyramid of the summit.

Odell's own plan was not to follow the crest of the ridge but to make a rather circuitous route outwards over the northern face. He was a geologist and wanted to examine the geological structure of the mountain. The lower part he had found was formed of a variety of gneisses. But the greater part of the upper half was composed mainly of highly altered limestones; with here and there in small amount light granitoid rocks which break across, or are interbedded with, all the other series. To the layman the significance of this statement is that Mount Everest must have once lain beneath the sea – another revelation of the mighty energy it embodies.

'The whole series', writes Odell, 'dips outward from the mountain at about 30 degrees, and since the general slope of this face, above 25,000 feet, is about 40 degrees to 45 degrees, the effect is to make a series of overlapping slabs nearly parallel with the slope, and presenting a number of little faces often up to 50 feet in height, which can be climbed, usually by an easy though steepish route, while most can be entirely circumvented. The rocks are not on the whole rotten in texture since they have been considerably hardened by the igneous intrusions of granitoid rocks. But the slabs are often sprinkled with debris from above, and when to this is added freshly fallen snow, the labour and toil of climbing at these altitudes may perhaps be imagined. It is not so much the technical difficulty as the awkwardness of uncertain footing on a slope not quite steep enough for the use of one's hands.'

It was from about halfway between the two highest camps that Odell caught that last glimpse of Mallory and Irvine which has already been described. He was surprised at their being so late in the day so far from the summit; and reflecting on the cause of this he continued his way up to Camp VI. On arrival there at about two o'clock snow commenced to fall and the wind increased. He placed his load of fresh provisions, etc., inside the tiny tent and took shelter for a while. Within was an assortment of spare clothes, scraps of food, two sleeping bags, oxygen cylinders and parts of apparatus. Outside were more parts of the apparatus and of the duralumin carriers. But the climbers had left no note, and Odell could know nothing therefore of the time of their departure or what might have intervened to cause delay.

Snow continued to fall, and, after a while, Odell began to

wonder whether the weather and conditions higher up might not compel the party to return. Camp VI – that is, this tiny tent – was in rather a concealed position on a ledge and backed by a small crag. In the prevailing conditions the returning party might experience considerable difficulty in finding it. So Odell went out in the direction of the summit, and having scrambled about 200 feet commenced whistling and yodelling in case they should happen to be within hearing. He then took shelter from the driving sleet behind a rock. He could not see more than a few yards ahead so thick was the atmosphere. And in an endeavour to forget the cold he examined the rocks about him. But in the flurry of snow and the biting wind even his ardour for geology began to wane, and within an hour he decided to turn back. Supposing that Mallory and Irvine were returning they could under existing conditions hardly yet be within call.

As he reached Camp VI the squall blew over, and before long the whole North Face became bathed in sunshine. The uppermost crags were distinctly seen. But of the climbers there was not a sign.

Odell was now in an awkward predicament. Every inclination would make him want to stay where he was or even go forward to meet his friends. But Mallory, in his last note, had particularly requested him to return to the North Col and be ready to evacuate Camp IV, and with himself and Irvine proceed to Camp III that same night, in case the monsoon should suddenly break. And the reason why Odell would have to go on ahead was that Camp VI, consisting of only one small tent, was incapable of holding more than two men. If he remained he would have to sleep outside. And to sleep outside at 27,000 feet meant only one thing.

Reluctantly, therefore, Odell was compelled to carry out Mallory's wishes. After partaking of a little food and leaving ample for them, he closed up the tent, and about 4.30 left the camp and made his way down by the extreme crest of the North-East Ridge. Halting now and then he would glance up and scan the upper rocks for any sign of the climbers. But he looked in vain. By then they should be well on their way down, but, even if they were, there was little hope of picking them out at that great distance and against such a broken background – unless, indeed, they should be crossing one of the infrequent patches of snow, as had happened in the morning, or be silhouetted on the crest of the ridge. By 6.15 he was abreast of Camp V, but there being no reason to turn aside to it he pressed on and was interested in finding that descending at high altitudes is little more fatiguing than descending at moderate altitudes. This gave him confidence that unless the climbers above were completely exhausted they would find themselves able to make faster time downward than they had expected and so escape being benighted. By means of a careful glissade Odell covered the distance between Camps V and IV in barely thirty-five minutes.

At the latter camp he was welcomed by Hazard with a wonderful brew of hot soup and plenty of tea. And being refreshed the two went out again to watch for Mallory and Irvine. The evening was clear and they watched till late that night but still there were no signs. They could conjecture that they must have been belated and hope that in the moonlight reflected from the surrounding peaks they might find their way to one or other of the upper camps.

The tiny tents of those two camps Odell scrutinized through

his field-glasses the next morning – June 9th – but no movement whatever could be seen. Now deeply anxious he decided once more to return to the mountain. He settled a code of signals with Hazard, using an arrangement of sleeping bags to be placed against the snow for use by day, and some simple flash lights by night. With some difficulty he persuaded two porters to come with him; and by 12.15 he started. On the way up he encountered that same bitter crosswind from the west which nearly always prevails and which made the two porters repeatedly falter. But he reached Camp V about half-past three. And here he had to spend the night, for there was no possibility of his being able to reach the higher camp that evening. There was, as he expected, no sign of Mallory and Irvine and the prospects were black indeed.

The weather also was black that night. Gusts of boisterous wind sweeping over the face of the mountain threatened bodily to uproot the two small tents from the slender security of the ledges and carry both tents and men down the mountain side. Fleeting glimpses of a stormy sunset could fitfully be seen through the flying scud. And as the night closed in both wind and cold increased. Thus aggravated by the wind the cold was so intense that Odell was unable to sleep and remained chilled, even inside two sleeping bags and with all his clothes on.

Morning broke with the wind as strong and the cold as bitter as ever. The two porters refused to be roused; they seemed to be suffering from extreme lassitude or nausea, and only made signs of being sick and wishing to descend. To proceed under the storm conditions about them was more than they could face. All Odell could do was to send them back. But he went on himself.

After seeing them well on their way downward he set off for Camp VI. And this time he took oxygen. He had found in the tent the oxygen apparatus which he had taken up there two days before, and he now carried it but with one cylinder only. He had not much faith in the use of oxygen, but he hoped that by using it he would make quicker time upward. In this, however, he was disappointed. The boisterous and bitter wind, blowing as ever from the west athwart the ridge, was trying in the extreme and he could only make slow progress. From time to time, in order to restore warmth, he would take shelter behind rocks or crouch low in some recess. But after about an hour he found he was deriving little good from the oxygen. Thinking this might be due to his taking it in only moderate quantities he gave himself more and with longer inspirations. Still, however, the effect was almost negligible – perhaps a trifle allayment in the tire of his legs. He was too well acclimatized to need it and he accordingly switched it off. He decided to proceed with the apparatus on his back but without the objectionable mouthpiece between his lips and depend on direct breathing from the atmosphere; and he seemed to get on quite as well though he was breathing at a rate which would surprise even a long-distance runner.

Thus pressing upward he at length reached Camp VI. There everything was as he had left it. There was not a sign of Mallory and Irvine. And that they had died on the mountain was now certain.

The question was how and when they had died, and if they had reached the summit before they died. In the faint but anxious hope of being able to find some trace of them in the limited time available Odell dumped the oxygen apparatus and immediately set off along the route which Mallory and Irvine would probably have taken in the descent – the crest of the ridge – where he had last seen them on their upward climb. But Everest was in its most forbidding aspect. A darkened atmosphere hid its features, and a gale raced over its cruel face. After struggling on for a couple of hours, looking in vain for a possible clue, he realized that the chances of finding any on such a vast expanse of crags and broken slabs was small indeed. And for any more extensive search towards the final pyramid a further party would have to be organized. In the time available it was impossible for him to extend his search. And only too reluctantly he made his way back to Camp VI.

Seizing the opportunity of a lull in the wind he, with great effort, dragged the two sleeping bags from the tents and up the precipitous rocks behind to a steep snow patch plastered on a bluff of rocks above. So boisterous still was the wind that it needed all his effort to cut steps up the steep snow slope and thus fix the bags in position. Placed in the shape of a T they formed the signal announcing to those 4000 feet below that no traces of their comrades could be found.

Having made the sad signal Odell returned to the tent, and after taking from it Mallory's compass and the oxygen set of Irvine's design, the only articles which seemed worth while to retrieve, he closed it up and prepared to return.

But before departing he glanced up at the mighty summit above him. Ever and anon it deigned to unveil its cloud-wreathed features. It seemed to look down in cold indifference on him, mere puny man; and, to his petition to yield up the secret of his friends, howl derision in gusts of wind. And yet, as he gazed again, another mood appeared to creep over her haunting features. There seemed to be something alluring in that towering presence. He was almost fascinated. He realized that any mountaineer must be thus fascinated; that he who approached close must ever be led on, and, oblivious of all obstacles, seek to reach that most sacred and highest place of all.

It seemed to Odell that his friends also must have been thus enchanted: for why else should they tarry. And perhaps this enchantment of the summit is the solution of the mystery. For a great mountain invites as well as defies; and the nearer the summit men reach the intenser is the attraction. The mountain will extract from him the last grain of energy and the last flicker of courage ere she yields to his persistence. She will compel his greatness out of man, and make him put forth more and more of himself. But for that very reason he is enchanted by her: she has made him be his best.

The mountain is like much else in this world. One of the great mysteries of existence is that what is most awful and most terrible does not deter man but draws him to it – to his temporary disaster, perhaps, but in the end to an intensity of joy which without the risk he could never have experienced.

Odell himself was evidently thus drawn, and if it had not been for the anxiety it would cause his companions he might have rested the night and struck out for the summit next day. And who knows but that he might have reached it, for he was the fittest who had yet been on the mountain.

That, however, was not to be, and once again he set forth down the mountain. Hampered by the unwieldy oxygen outfit which he had no need to use but wished to recover in memory of his friends, and buffeted by storm blasts that seemed to pierce him through and through, all his attention was needed to negotiate safely the exposed slabs of the ridge and prevent a slip on their debris-sprinkled surfaces. He quickened his pace on the easier ground further down, but at times found it necessary to seek protection from the biting gale in the lee of rocks and assure himself that he had no symptoms of frostbite. At length he reached the North Col Camp and was relieved to find a note from Norton and to discover that he had anticipated Norton's wishes not to prolong his stay upon the mountain in view of the imminent approach of the monsoon. He might perhaps have reached the summit, but storms might have prevented his ever getting back. No support was now available. And he might have only added one more to the already heavy list of casualties.

He could have done none other than return: he owed that to his comrades. Still there will ever be the haunting enchantment of the summit and the recurrent surmise that he might have attained it.

Chapter Twenty-Seven

THE GREAT ENIGMA

The great question remains: Did Mallory and Irvine reach the summit?

When last seen by Odell they were considerably behind time. It was 12.50, and they were then at least eight hundred feet from the summit, and possibly a thousand. Odell is not perfectly certain of the exact spot on the mountain at which he saw them. It was only a hurried glimpse of them he had through the unveiling of the mountain by the billowing mists; and on the broken rugged crest of a ridge it is not easy to be certain of the position. In any case, they were much below where Mallory had expected to be at that time. Indeed, he had hoped to be on the summit by then.

We have first then to examine the possible reasons for the delay to see if there was anything in them to make us think that the climbers would not be able to reach the summit. Odell has gone into this matter thoroughly. It will be recalled that the day of Mallory's ascent was not fine as it was when Norton and Somervell made their supreme effort. It was squally and misty. Odell, 2000 feet below, had experienced boisterous wind and bitter cold and thick driving mist. And when this mist cleared for a moment and he had that wonderful glimpse of the summit he had noticed that there was a considerable quantity of new snow covering some of the upper rocks near the topmost ridge. This may have been one of the causes of their delay. Another may have been the weight and unwieldiness of the oxygen apparatus. Mallory in his very last note – that from Camp VI – had inveighed against it as a nasty load for climbing. He used in fact a stronger word than nasty. And burdened with this clumsy apparatus the snow-covered debris-sprinkled slabs may have given much trouble. Then again the oxygen apparatus itself may have needed repair or readjustment, either before or after they left Camp VI, and this may have delayed them. It is just conceivable, also, though rather unlikely, that the zone of mist and clouds which Odell had experienced may have extended up to their level and so have somewhat impeded their progress.

Any or all of these factors, says Odell, may have hindered them and prevented their getting higher in the time. But when he saw them 'they were moving expeditiously as if endeav-ouring to make up for lost time'. And the word 'expeditiously' is particularly to be noted.

So it comes to this that at 12.50 they were eight hundred or perhaps a thousand feet from the summit. And four o'clock being the latest time at which they should arrive there and yet leave sufficient time to return in safety to camp – both Mallory and Norton were agreed on this point – could they in those three hours climb that height?

It would mean climbing at the rate of rather under or rather over 300 feet an hour according to the position in which they actually were when Odell saw them. Norton and Somervell

THE EPIC OF MOUNT EVEREST

without oxygen had not been able to attain this speed. Between Camp VI and the highest point they reached their rate of progress had been only 205 feet per hour. But with oxygen they might have been able to move quicker and, as we have noted, when Odell saw them they were moving expeditiously. A rate of 300 feet an hour might therefore be expected of them, and a much faster rate than that is possible.

But they may have encountered some serious obstacle on the way to the summit and be balked at the last moment? This is improbable. There seemed to Odell to be only two places which might in any way cause them trouble. The first was what the expedition knew as the 'second step'. This seemed steep but was negotiable on its north side. The second place that might have presented any difficulty is at the very foot of the final pyramid, where the slabs steepen before the relatively easy-looking ridge to the final summit can be attained. Norton had already observed that at this point caution would be specially necessary. But, as Odell remarks, such moderate difficulties as this part presents cannot long have detained a leader of Mallory's experience and skill, much less defeated him. So there was really no physical obstacle to prevent their reaching the summit.

The oxygen apparatus may have failed, of course, and thus have reduced them to the rate at which Norton and Somervell climbed. But, in Odell's opinion, the stoppage of oxygen would not have caused their complete collapse: he himself when using oxygen on the way from Camp V to Camp VI had switched it off at about 26,000 feet and had continued on, and returned, without using it; Mallory and Irvine were using only very little and they had both during the previous weeks spent adequate time at extreme altitudes, namely 21,000 feet and over, to become sufficiently acclimatized and not liable to collapse in the event of the oxygen failing.

The remaining possible cause which might have prevented their reaching the summit is an accident. A slip is always possible in the case of the most experienced mountaineers; and from his own observation of the rock in the neighbourhood of the point where they were last seen a serious slip for one of a roped party of two might spell destruction for both; and more particularly would this be so when – as on the day in question – these sloping slabs are covered with a thick powdering of fresh snow.

All or any of these causes may have prevented Mallory and Irvine reaching the summit; but it is also possible that they may not have stopped them from reaching the summit but did prevent them from returning to safety in Camp VI. They may have stood on the summit but met with mishap on the way back. Norton and all the others, except Odell, attribute their failure to return to a slip. But that slip may have occurred on the way down. And it is more likely to have occurred then when they were more exhausted, yet moving more quickly, and perhaps a trifle more carelessly owing to their elation, than on their way up.

They may have reached the summit later even than four o'clock. Down below, according to Norton, Mallory had most definitely made up his mind that as leader of a party the responsibility lay heavy on him 'to turn back, however near the summit, in good time to ensure a return to safety'.

'*However near the summit!*' But did even Mallory compute aright the enchantment of the summit? He knew well how

Everest could repel. Did he equally realize how she could attract? Did he appraise aright his own susceptibility to the charms of the summit at close hand? Say he was actually on the final pyramid; say he was only a couple of hundred feet in height, and less than two hundred yards in distance, from the summit, and that his watch showed him that it was four o'clock; would he forthwith put it back in his pocket and turn his steps downward? And even if he himself had that superhuman self-control would his younger companion have the same? Wouldn't Irvine have said, 'I don't care what happens. I'm going to have my fling for the top.' And could Mallory then have held out any longer? Wouldn't he rather have given in with joyous relief?

This certainly is a view which some will hold. And it is what Odell held. As he himself had been brought under the spell of the summit, so it seemed to him must his friends have been enchanted also. 'In action', he says of Mallory, 'the desire to overcome may have been too strong for him. The knowledge of his own proved powers of endurance, and those of his companion, may have urged him to make a bold bid for the summit . . . And who of us that has wrestled with some Alpine giant in the teeth of a gale, or in a race with the darkness, could hold back when such a victory, such a triumph of human endeavour, was within our grasp?'

Odell thinks then that there is a strong probability that Mallory and Irvine succeeded – that they reached the summit but were benighted on their return.

In that case they might have been expected to use the light signals they had with them? But they may have forgotten they had them; or not thought of using them; or, still more likely, may have been withheld by chivalry from signalling. They must have known that a signal could only drag Odell from the North Col for a second time up to 27,000 feet, and beyond that, to almost certain death. No one could be up in time to be of avail. No – they had made their supreme effort and whether they returned or not men could be sure that they had done their utmost. And in that assurance they must have died.

Where and when they died we know not. But there in the arms of Mount Everest they lie for ever – lie 10,000 feet above where any man has lain in death before. Everest indeed conquered their bodies. But their spirit is undying. No man onward from now will ever climb a Himalayan peak and not think of Mallory and Irvine.

Chapter Twenty-Eight

HONOUR

News of the tragedy spread at once all over the world and everywhere sympathy was evoked. The King sent messages of condolence to the climbers' families and to the expedition and asked a member of the Mount Everest Committee to give him all available particulars. His Majesty especially wished to know how the accident had occurred. For at first it was generally supposed that there had been an accident. Only a very brief telegram had been dispatched by Norton at first, as a lengthy telegram with a full account was to follow. Nothing was known of a final attempt having been made to reach the summit; and it was generally assumed that Mallory and Irvine had lost their lives in some accident on the mountain – probably on the dangerous North Col.

It came then with a sense of relief – almost of triumph – when Norton's full telegram arrived telling how they had almost reached the summit and that Norton himself and Somervell had reached the 28,000 feet level and something over. Their lives had not been given in vain. Something memorable had been achieved.

Messages of sympathy and condolence came to the Alpine

Club and Royal Geographical Society from mountaineering clubs all over the world. Memorial services were held at Birkenhead, which happened to be the home of both Mallory and Irvine, and at Magdalene College, Cambridge, and at Merton College, Oxford. And, mainly on the initiative of Douglas Freshfield, a national memorial service was held in St Paul's Cathedral when the expedition had returned home.

At this service the King, Queen Alexandra, the Prince of Wales, the Duke of York, Prince Arthur of Connaught were all represented. And it was attended by General Bruce, Colonel Norton and nearly all the members of the three expeditions, by the President and most of the council of the Royal Geographical Society, and by the Committee and many members of the Alpine Club. There was also a large congregation of the general public. The Dean of St Paul's himself read the lessons. And an address was given, at the special request of the Mount Everest Committee, by the Bishop of Chester (Dr Paget) in whose diocese Mallory's father was a rector.

The bishop so well expressed the mind and feelings of those who took part in and of those who were responsible for the Everest expeditions that his words were published in the *Geographical Journal* for December, 1924, and may be repeated here. He took as his text the words, 'In whose heart are Thy ways', and said:

'Many no doubt know what stands for these words in the Latin version of the Psalms; a version used even more largely than ours, and more familiar in its beauty to a vast number of fellow-Christians – *Ascensiones in corde suo disposuit*: He has set ascents in his heart; or, as we would phrase it, He has set his heart on ascents.

'It meant for the psalmist no steep or dangerous climb. It meant at most a long and tedious journey, the sort of thing that is a venturesome undertaking to a quiet soul who lives at far distance from the temple and city of God. But it led him upwards, it led him to the place he wished to reach. Whether in memory or in anticipation, the road was dear to him. He had set his heart on it: he loved the upward path. It was fixed in his affection. *Ascensiones in corde suo disposuit.*

'Far different from that easy pilgrimage is the challenge of the heights which has drawn into closest fellowship many of those who are here today. A great unanimity gives intense significance to your assembling in the house of God. For the lovers of the heights are a brotherhood more intimate, more closely united, more affectionately disposed to one another than almost any other group of men. It is as natural as it is beautiful that before your great meeting this evening you should meet here to remember, as in God's presence, those whose names are written in your records in letters of gold.

'It is not for us timid pedestrians to pretend that we understand your love of the heights. But if even from a distance and from some miserably lower level we have looked from afar upon the mountains, or known the silence of the snowfields, and the widening vision, and the exhilarating keenness of the air, and the perfect azure of the skies (and you are good enough to believe that even the humblest may breathe the spirit of the mountains), can anyone wonder at the fascination those mountains have for the real climber, that you have so set in your hearts the love of the heights? *Ascensiones in corde suo disposuit.* Might it not almost be the motto of the Alpine Club?

'It is simply because they both came from our country and

diocese of Chester that I am asked to speak today. I am bidden, so far as such a thing is possible, to represent the homes from which they come, and those who love them best. They, I am sure, understand and value very highly what you wish to express by your presence. They are grateful to you for it. I got them to tell me something of the boyhood and early years of their glorious sons. In each instance there was the like story of quiet modest strength, of infinite perseverance, of a great and tender love of home, of a transparent purity of heart, of the deep and simple things that make fathers and mothers very thankful and very proud. I wish you could have been with us at Birkenhead, where, nearer home, an assembly not less significant, though it may be less august than this, tried to show its love for them and theirs.

'And as we read what was so lovingly written, with all the eloquence of its reserve, it was not difficult to see in it the presage of what was to follow at Winchester and Shrewsbury, at Cambridge and Oxford, in the Alps and in Spitzbergen, and at last on Mount Everest. It was the same Leigh Mallory who veiled the grace and brilliance of his leadership under the impenetrable cloak of his modesty; who when something like disaster occurred insisted on claiming responsibility for it, and when an incredible presence of mind on his part saved the lives of others never let us know that it was he; who reminded us that in a matter like this we are all comrades! Yes, and the same Andrew Irvine who, with all his brilliant, his amazing, his premature attainments as a climber, would laugh as he set himself to the humblest task, or use the splendour of his giant strength to bear the burdens of other men.

'*Ascensiones in corde suo disposuit.* Was it only love of high

THE EPIC OF MOUNT EVEREST

mountains that was set in hearts like these? No; but rather that with the love of the mountains was the ascent of spiritual altitudes, splendid peaks of courage and unselfishness and cheerfulness, such as are reached not necessarily by the sure-footed and clear-headed, but always by the compassionate, the brotherly, and the pure in heart.

'For indeed the record of Mount Everest may well help men, if not to feel the mystery of the mountain, yet surely to enter more deeply, more reverently, into the spirit of the mountaineer.

'Thankful as we are for what the expedition has to tell us of the way and the attempts and the great achievement and for its marvellous pictures, it is perhaps as a human record and a human document that it speaks most clearly and speaks to us in St Paul's today. The indomitable cheerfulness, the amazing courage of it, the passion for work, the refusal of praise. You have indeed set *Ascensiones* in our hearts: you have helped us more than you think to see those things which are above; Whatsoever things are true and honourable, just and pure, lovely and of good report, if there be any manly virtue, if there be any praise, you have helped us to think on these things.

'George Mallory, Andrew Irvine, lovely and pleasant in their lives, in death were not divided.

'It seems as though when God means us to learn He is wont to clothe that by which He teaches us in some form of simple and solemn beauty, of which it is hard to mistake or resist the appeal. So it is here! The cloud clears away for a moment and you are allowed to see the two men making, steadily and strongly, for the summit. That is the last you see of them, and the question as to their reaching the summit is still unanswered; it will be solved some day. The merciless mountain gives no reply!

'But that last ascent, with the beautiful mystery of its great enigma, stands for more than an heroic effort to climb a mountain, even though it be the highest in the world – *Sic itur ad astra*.

'Think of it how you will: as the ascent by which the kingly spirit goes up to the House of the Lord; as the ascent through death to endless life; as the ascent by which the men of clean hands and pure hearts ascend into the hill of the Lord and rise up in His holy place; as the way He went who said, "I go to prepare a place for you, that where I am there ye may be also."

> Lofty designs must end in like effects,
> Loftily lying,
> Leave them – still loftier than the world suspects,
> Living and dying.

For they indeed go from strength to strength, who have set their hearts on the heights.'

On the same evening, October 17th, that this service in St Paul's took place, a joint meeting of the Royal Geographical Society and the Alpine Club, with Lord Ronaldshay, the President of the former, in the chair, was held in the Albert Hall and addressed by General Bruce, Norton, Odell, and Geoffrey Bruce. The hall was filled to its capacity; and that those who were prevented from joining in the memorial service in the morning might join in the tribute of admiration and respect which was then paid to their memory, Lord

Ronaldshay asked all to show their respect in silence by rising in their places.

Thus did England honour her sons.

Mallory was only a Cambridge lecturer, and Irvine an Oxford undergraduate;

But they had brought honour to her and she did honour to them;

And their name will be ever remembered.

Chapter Twenty-Nine

THE DOOMED MOUNTAIN

By reaching so near the summit the 1924 expedition proved that to climb the highest mountain in the world is a feasible proposition. The mountain presents no insuperable physical obstacles; and man has proved that he has the physical capacity to climb even this earth's greatest height. Why not leave it at that? With the knowledge now obtained the needs of science are satisfied. Should not further efforts be abandoned?

Whatever reason may answer to that question – whatever wisdom may have to say – it is certain that spirit will answer an emphatic No. No, the attempt should *not* be abandoned. Knowledge is not everything in life. Science may be satisfied, but the soul is not. It was the spirit, not science, that embarked upon this enterprise. And the spirit can never rest satisfied until it is completed.

If any men have the right to speak the fatal word 'Abandon', it is the men who stood so near the summit, who knew well all the risks and hardships, and who had suffered the loss of their comrades. Yet it is these very men – and these very men with their fearful experiences fresh on them – who first said, 'Try again'. Abandonment to them was unthinkable. On their way back from the mountain they cabled urging that another attempt should be made. Loyalty to their dead comrades demanded it. And before they had reached India they had deliberately seated themselves down and written out the results of their experiences in every detail of organization for the benefit of the *next* expedition.

For the moment, the arrangements which the Mount Everest Committee had contemplated for a fourth expedition, are in abeyance because of the difficulty of obtaining leave from the Tibetan government. These wise Tibetans think that merely to climb a mountain cannot be the true object of these huge expeditions coming out from England year after year, always commanded by generals and colonels, never reaching the summit, but always prying about round the mountain, and always taking a look into Nepal. And whatever they do in the mountain the gods are clearly displeased, for thirteen of the climbers have already been killed at their hands. Better refuse further permission than risk political trouble or the fury of the outraged gods of the mountain. While this is the attitude of the Tibetans permission is hard to obtain. For the present the Tibetans stand in the path. And they may stand there for years yet. But in the end man will have his way. Another and another expedition will be sent to Mount Everest, and with the certitude of mathematics man will prevail.

The mountain now stands there proud and erect and unconquered. And the faint-hearted peoples around it fear to approach it. They have the capacity of body to reach the summit any year they liked. But they are lacking in spirit. All they attain to is the painting of pictures depicting the fierce anger of gods repelling the English who dared to approach them. For all that the mountain is doomed. Man knows the worst about it. He knows exactly the way by which he can creep up it. He knows the extremes of frost and snow and tempest that defend it. But he knows also that the mountain remains stationary in capacity for defence while he is increasing in capacity to conquer. The mountain cannot increase in height or have severer cold or more tempestuous winds to defend it. But man, when he next comes, will be very different from what he was when last there. He will come with increased knowledge, increased experience, and increased spirit. Knowing that a camp has already been carried to nearly 27,000 feet he will carry a camp well beyond that height. Now that he has once got past 28,000 feet the remaining eight or nine hundred will not affright him. Fifty years back he had not ascended higher than 21,000. Then he climbed to 23,000. Then to 24,600. Then to 27,000. Then to 28,000. He clearly could not fail to reach the final 29,000.

This seems all the more certain if we consider Odell's performance. Odell had experienced quite as much of the pains as Everest is ever likely to inflict on man. He had not gone through the extra strain of rescuing the porters. But he had endured the suffering of the excessive cold and the blizzard. He may therefore be taken as an example of what a climber can do against the worst that Everest can do. And this is his record.

Between May 31st and June 11th he went three times up and down between 21,000 feet and 23,000 feet. This would have been thought quite a noteworthy performance in itself before these Everest expeditions were launched. But 23,000 feet had now come to be considered only the starting point; and it is his performances from this point onward that are so remarkable.

Twice he climbed to the 26,800 feet camp and a little beyond, and once, in addition, to the 25,200 feet camp; and the two ascents to about the 27,000-feet level were made in four consecutive days. During the last ascent he carried heavy oxygen apparatus, but only used the oxygen for about an hour; and the ascent was made in a raging wind. Another feature of Odell's performance is that during twelve days he spent only one night below 23,000 feet; and two he spent at 25,000 feet.

Now supposing that on the crucial day when Mallory and Irvine started for the top and Odell reached Camp VI, 26,800 feet, he had stopped the night there instead of descending to the Base Camp; and supposing that he had the next day gone for the summit, is it not practically certain that he would have got there? As it was, he returned that same day to Camp IV and the next day to Camp V and the day after (with a heavy oxygen apparatus) to Camp VI, and back to Camp IV. If he could do that – if he could go down from 27,000 feet to 23,000 feet and back again to 27,000 – is it not fairly certain that he could have gone from 27,000 feet to 29,000 feet?

In any case, what Odell did, added to what Norton and Somervell achieved in climbing to an altitude of 28,100 feet and 28,000 feet respectively (also without oxygen); and added also to what the sturdy porters had done in twice carrying loads to nearly the 27,000-feet level confirms and amplifies the discovery made on the previous expedition and shows that man possesses the power of adapting himself to the conditions prevailing at the highest altitudes. His bodily organism does not remain fixed and unalterable. It rises to meet the new call made upon it by the strange surroundings and is able to do what before that adaptation took place had seemed impossible.

And again it was found that his mind like the body rises to the occasion and adapts itself to the new conditions. After a higher level had once been reached the mind accepted the fact and the acceptance of it made the attainment of a still higher level more easy. This was notably the case when the porters for a second time carried loads to about the 27,000-feet level. The mind had no longer to trouble itself with the question whether the feat was possible or not; the thing had been done. And with the accomplishment of higher and higher achievements the mind more readily adapted itself to the attainment of the supreme end. Once again man learned that the more he tries the more he can do.

Without doubt, then, one day man will conquer the mountain. But in that great day he who first stands on the summit, with the whole mountain beneath his feet, will be the surest to feel and quickest to acknowledge what he owes to those pioneers who made his victory possible. His name it may be which will go down to posterity as having first climbed the highest mountain in the world. But with it should ever be associated the names of Mallory and Irvine, of Norton, Somervell and Odell, and also of Napboo Yishay, Lhakpa Chedi, and Semchumbi, those stout-hearted and sturdy-bodied porters who first showed that a camp could be carried to within reach of the summit.

Probably not a single one of those who took part in the last expedition will be able to join the next. The more necessary is it, then, that young men with ambition for climbing should prepare themselves to gain the great prize. The Mount Everest

Committee is still 'in being' to help men to win it. And when the committee are in a position to make the next call may there be those who are fit as well as ready to respond. For Everest will accept defeat from none but the fittest in body, mind, and spirit.

Besides Everest, there are in the Himalaya no less than seventy-four peaks over 24,000 feet in height; and not one of them has been climbed to the top. Men have ascended to great heights on their sides, but not attained the summit of one. The Everest expeditions, though they have failed in their main object, have at least proved this: that there is nothing in the effects of altitude alone to prevent a climber attaining the summit of any one of these lesser peaks. And if men set themselves to climbing them, they will not only be fitting themselves for the eventual struggle with Everest, but will also be opening up a whole new world of beauty, inexhaustible in extent, and to be enjoyed for the labour of seeking.

And in seeking may they carry the Himalayan peoples with them. May the sacrifices made in rescuing the porters on the North Col have not been in vain. May the fellowship with these peoples which Bruce founded, and which Norton, Somervell, and Mallory sealed, be maintained and developed; so that when the next assault is delivered on Everest the climbers may count on the loyal and willing comradeship of these sturdy Himalayans, and success be assured.